The Media
2nd Edition

Brian Dutton

Head of Humanities,
Palmers College, Grays, Essex

 LONGMAN

Addison Wesley Longman Limited
Edinburgh Gate, Harlow
Essex CM20 2JE, England
and Associated Companies throughout the World

ISBN 0 582 28808 8

First published 1971
Second edition 1997
Produced by Longman Singapore Published Pte Ltd
Printed in Singapore

The Publisher's policy is to use paper manufactured from sustainable forests.

Acknowledgements

We are grateful to the following for permission to reproduce copyright material:

the author, Professor S Hall for an extract from his article 'Mugging; a case study of the media' pp571–572 *The Listener* (1.5.75); Newspaper Publishing Plc for the article 'TV-addict children "lack concentration"' by Fran Abrams from *The Independent* 1.6.96; Pluto Press for an extract from *On Television* by Stuart Hood (1980); Routledge for an extract and table from *What News? The market, Politics and the Local Press* by Bob Franklin and David Murphy (Routledge, 1991) and for extracts from *Understanding* News by J Hartley (Methuen, 1982) and *Media Culture* by Douglas Kellner (Routledge, 1985); Dave Thomas for an extract from his article in *The Best of the Football Fanzines* (Pubd. by Soccer Book Publishing Ltd).

We are also grateful to the following for permission to reproduce photographs and other copyright material:

The Arts Council of England, page 3; Ros Asquith, page 68; Mick Kidd © BIFF, page 103; *BROADCAST* 23.2.96/BARB, page 88–89; Broadcasting Standards Council, page 69; Living in Britain: Results from the 1994 General Household Survey (1996), Office for National Statistics. Crown Copyright 1996. Reproduced by permission of the Controller of HMSO and of the Office for National Statistics, page 81; Express Newspapers plc, page 75; Reprinted by permission of Fourth Estate Ltd from *The Media Guide 1996*, edited by Steve Peak & Paul Fisher © 1995 Guardian News Service & Steve Peak, page 24; *Frontline* (photo: Juan Aparicio), page 86; © 1995 Future Publishing Ltd, page 93; Glasgow Media Group, page 65; Harvey Nicols & Co Ltd/Kobal, page 13; *Intermedia*, The Journal of the International Institute of Communcations. News Agenda Survey 1992, page 99; LADD Co/Warner Brothers (courtesy Kobal), page 46; MGM/Pathe (courtesy Kobal), page 72; from Alastair Hetherington, *News, Newspapers & Television*, Macmillan Ltd 1985, page 58; National Readership Survey 1995, page 104 above; News International Newspapers Ltd, page 5; *Premiere* May 1996, page 23; *Radiohead World Service Fanzine*, page 87; Radio Joint Audience Research Ltd, page 104 below; Sony UK Ltd, page 14; Yves Saint Laurent, page 50.

Contents

Introduction

The aim of this book is to provide a concise and accessible introduction to some of the main concepts and issues which arise from the study of the media in contemporary society. In updating the first edition, I have tried to incorporate some of the more significant developments which have shaped the media in recent years and also reflect some of the newer academic approaches to the study of the media such as post-modernism.

The opening chapter includes a survey of the main areas of debate and how these have evolved in the last half century or more. Chapter 2 focuses on the production of the media and what factors help determine the nature of what is produced. The actual content and meaning of media representation is the theme of Chapter 3. This is probably the most contentious area of media debate and is inextricably tied to the role of media audiences and how they interpret the media, which is discussed in the final chapter of the book.

The most tentative conclusions within the book are to be found in Chapter 4 on new technologies. If there is one certainty in studying the media, it is that the constant flow of social and technological change means that the future development and cultural role of the media is very unpredictable. At this point of time, it would seem reasonable to claim that the media's importance as a form of cultural communication is likely to become even more significant as we move into the 21st century. I hope this book will serve as a stimulating introduction to the study of the media, and for those wishing to pursue more in-depth analyses of the issues raised in the book, there are suggestions for further reading at the end of Chapter 5.

1 The media and popular culture

What are the media?

'The media' is a term which forms part of the vocabulary of everyday conversation in modern society. Although rarely made explicit, the word 'media' is commonly understood to refer to print (principally newspapers, magazines and comics) and electronic audio-visual (principally television, radio, cinema and music) forms of communication. However, in practice it is not possible to delineate precisely what constitutes communication forms which qualify for the term 'the media'.

One strategy for identifying the relevant technological terrain is to define the principal characteristics of media communication. These could be said to include:

1 an ability to reach a large number of people simultaneously (hence the frequently used prefix *mass* media). Therefore the media are both *popular* and *immediately accessible*.
2 the employment of high technology to facilitate communication on such a scale. For example, the World Cup Final is relayed live to several hundred million viewers via satellite television.
3 a distinction between a relatively closed and centralised source of production and a public and dispersed site of reception.
4 communication in which there is little direct interaction between source and receiver. Because of the technology, all of the communication effectively involves *mediation*. Unlike face-to-face contact, media sources seem remote and invisible so that audience responses are qualitatively different. We can only physically respond through the media technology itself.

Despite listing such criteria, there are still forms and practices of communication whose qualifying status for inclusion within the media is problematic. Popular paperback fiction is a serious contender but is compromised because of its lack of immediacy. Popular music would seem to qualify by virtue of its dissemination through radio, television, etc., but is not easily separable from more 'serious' or established musical styles lacking popular recognition or appeal. [4]

Further ambiguity has been created by the spread of electronic mail (especially the Internet) and the adoption of video technology such as home shopping and videogames. It is not always clear how or if new technologies will become utilised as means of communication until they become established and recognised, or simply marginalised as a peripheral trend.

To try to clarify the issue of how to define and recognise the media I would wish to emphasise their status as a principal *social* and *cultural institution* in contemporary societies.

That is to say that the media comprise a socially recognised and structured form of communication which is technologically mediated. This, in turn, generates distinctive patterns of social relationships, routines and cultural meaning.

Why study the media?

As the academic study of the media has steadily grown in recent years, there has been a corresponding critical reaction which has questioned the legitimacy of such study. This critical response has been largely based on the assumption that media culture lacks any real educational value as it is mainly disposable, undemanding and shallow in nature. In contrast, works of 'high' culture deserve curriculum space because of their artistic worth, depth and longevity, e.g. classical music, art and literature.

While there may be an *aesthetic* argument which underpins a hierarchical ranking of cultural products, the main justification for studying media culture is its very *popularity*.

The statistics in Fig. 1.1 show that, for the majority of the population, participation in activities which might be called artistic or high culture is low, whereas virtually everyone regularly engages with some form of media activity. Rather than being a special occasion, the media form part of our everyday life in the same way as going shopping or going to work or school fits into our routine schedules.

Even if we consciously choose to ignore the media, it is very difficult to avoid some daily contact with media output such as advertising posters, radio broadcasts in shops, newspaper billboards, etc. It seems fair to say that modern society is characterised by *media saturation*, that is, the media permeate all walks of life and, indeed, for most people, are actively chosen as a form of information, stimulation or entertainment. Therefore, the media's very ubiquity – its sense of being all around us, is a principal justification for academic analysis.

Figure 1.1   Number of adults in England who attend arts events 1987/88 to 1995/96

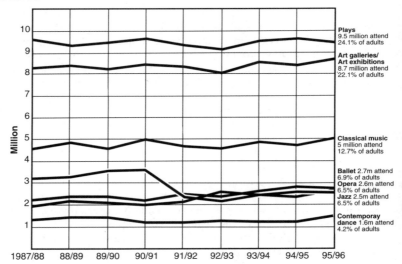

Source: Arts Council Annual Report 1995/96.

The figures are based on the number of people who said they either would attend or have attended concerts, plays, etc., during the year.

For the media the following data reflect the extent of audience activity.

Television viewing

Weekly reach	96%	*(BARB Feb 1996)*
Average hours of viewing per week	27.5	

Radio listening

Weekly reach	86%	*(RAJAR April 1996)*
Average hours of listening per week	21.6	

Newspaper readership

National morning newspaper	58%	*(NRS 1996)*
National Sunday newspaper	66%	

Magazine readership

Any general weekly magazine	43%	*(NRS 1996)*
Any general monthly magazine	48%	

Cinema attendance

% aged 7 or over claiming		
"to ever go" to the cinema	68%	*(Cinema Advertising Association 1995)*

While there is a sound educational case for studying the plays of William Shakespeare, there is an equally valid educational case for studying a daily newspaper like *The Sun*. Although few people voluntarily choose to read or see Shakespeare's plays, their accepted literary merit renders them an appropriate subject for close scrutiny. On the other hand, few would ascribe much literary merit to *The Sun*. However, for the last 20 years it has been Britain's best selling daily newspaper with an average readership of over 10 million per issue. Furthermore, it contributes significantly to the social and political discourse of contemporary British culture.

The front page in Fig. 1.2 refers to the 1992 general election when the Conservative Party won by a very slender margin after a strong anti-Labour campaign in most of the tabloid newspapers including *The Sun* (for a further discussion see page 109–110).

As the media do form such an important part of popular culture, it is not surprising that they have become the focus of increasing attention, and not just from academics. Politicians, church leaders, royalty, teachers and judges are but a few who regularly voice opinions about the media and are most critical of its effects (while, at the same time, not hesitating to use it to channel their protests).

As far back as 1970, James Halloran recorded the following observation concerning television,

'Television has been criticised for producing conformity, for operating in the interests of political and economic vested interest, for maintaining the status quo, diminishing the power and habit of critical thinking, concentrating on the trivial and sensational, standing in the way of a truly participatory democracy, producing a deterioration in aesthetic taste and general cultural standards and for nullifying hard won social gains, particularly in education ... '

The areas of debate

In seeking to analyse and make sense of the media, a wide range of theoretical and conceptual approaches have been utilised to date. These include sociology, cultural studies, structuralism, linguistics, psychology and literary analysis. In order to simplify what seems a bewildering array of academic avenues into studying the media, I have identified four main issues which have been the focus of interest.

Figure 1.2

Source: *The Sun*, 11 April 1992.

1   The media and society

Sociologists have tended to address the media in terms of its situation in the wider society, particularly its *structural* role or function. The critical theoretical tradition in sociology has its roots in Marxist theory which sees the media as a device for *social control* by those in power – for Marxists, the ruling or capitalist class who own the means of production. Taking a broader sociological perspective, other powerful groups may be identified based on gender (patriarchy) or race/ethnicity. Media production is in the hands of powerful groups, whose interests are protected through media content which presents the world in an *ideological* way.

Traditional functionalist sociologists have tended to view the media as having an *integrative* role, maintaining consensus through reinforcing central values in a way which is beneficial to society. In particular, American functionalists, such as Daniel Bell, have stressed the importance of the media in helping to shape Western societies as democracies in which all can participate and be informed.

A closely related perspective is that of *pluralism* which derives principally from an analysis of the distribution of power in society. It shares with functionalism a belief that the media aid democracy and meet the needs and interests of its consumers while recognising that modern society does not comprise a unity or consensus but, rather, has many competing interest groups struggling to gain their ends. This diversity of opinion is reflected in the wide range of media products available on the market. That 'supply meets demand in the free market' is the essence of the pluralist theory of the media.

2   Production

There is a popular view that it is the technology of the media, the means by which messages pass from their source to the audience, which is the all-powerful force at work. This is reflected in   Marshall McLuhan's maxim that 'the medium is the message'. Few, if any, sociologists adopt this line of thought, as to do so is to ignore the complex social, economic and political processes which help to shape media production. For example, Britons travelling to America are usually bewildered by the diet programmes that   American television has to offer, while Americans visiting Britain are equally perplexed at the content of the popular tabloid newspapers on sale over here.

For Marxists, ownership of the means of production is ultimately the determining factor in the analysis of any social practice. In this case, ownership of the media is seen as a key element in the mental domination of the capitalist class over the rest of society. Rather than a free market, where each group's interests are supplied by a wide variety of media outlets, Marxists argue that, just as in the business world in general, there is an ever-decreasing number of owners and a tightening grip on the market by the large multinational corporations.

Within the debate about whether there is still a ruling class in industrial societies, the ownership versus control of business argument is prominent. Do not the managers, who have no shares in companies but are merely employees, really control modern industry with their professional expertise and skill? The same question is raised about the media professionals who 'manage' and 'control' television and newspaper production. Those favouring an interactionist approach have looked at professionals working in media organisations (not forgetting that in Britain the BBC does not answer to any shareholders but is publicly owned) and suggested that professional autonomy may exist in large business corporations in a way which suggests that the Marxist view is unduly deterministic.

Another line of attack is from the pluralists who cite the persistence of smaller independent media outlets to cater for interests which might be seen as anti-capitalist, such as left-wing journals or critical television series (the controversy over some early Channel 4 programmes aimed at 'minority groups' is a typical example). Those readers who follow the pop/rock business will be aware of the success of independent record labels which periodically capture the market with new developments in music before usually being taken over by the large established labels. These issues are discussed in Chapter 2, but to some extent their resolution depends upon an examination of media products.

3 Representations

What kind of picture of the world is constructed by the media has been a central concern for those studying the media. Particularly influential has been the Marxist perspective which has argued that the interests of the ruling class are maintained through the media reproducing a *dominant ideology*, a set of beliefs and ideas which represent those interests as natural. Others adopting this critical line on media content perceive the media to reflect ideologies of gender, race and age which perpetuate these inequalities in the wider society.

In supporting these claims, early studies of media content emphasised the biased nature of news coverage or the misrepresentation of social groups through stereotyping or distortion. Evidence tended to be gathered through *content analysis*, whereby media content would be systematically studied and quantified and then compared to social reality in order to discover how (in)accurate media representations were.

Employing different techniques for analysing representations has been *semiology* which focuses on the meaning of signs – the constituent parts of language. In the case of the media, this means closely studying the way meaning is generated through two sets of signs (or codes):

1 the technical codes specific to media language, e.g. framing, lighting and sound in film and television
2 the cultural codes, including the whole range of subject matter such as dress, setting, characterisation, narrative, etc.

Collectively, these signs constitute media *texts* like films, magazines and advertisements whose meaning can be *decoded* through close textual analysis. Another way of putting it is that every media text constructs meaning through combinations of signs (or signifying practices), then, in order to arrive at these meanings, we have to *deconstruct* the text. How the media construct representations of social reality is the theme of Chapter 3.

4 Audiences

Given that signs are capable of being interpreted in more than one way (they rarely have a culturally fixed meaning), this has consequences for the degree of uncertainty or ambiguity that exists in analysing representations constructed by media texts. Within semiological terms, media texts are *polysemic* – they may be 'read' in more than one way. Therefore, in order to pursue what meanings are contained within media texts, we need to consider the role of the audience as active reader or interpreter.

This is a radically different emphasis from that which seeks to examine how audiences are affected or influenced by media content. Much sociological and psychological research has been undertaken to measure or demonstrate the power of the media over the audience, and although the notion of a simple one-way cause and effect relationship is now considered overly simplistic, there is still a widespread assumption that the balance of power between media 'producers' and audiences is unequal. The role of the audience is considered in Chapter 4.

How the debate has evolved

In the last section of this introduction, I would like to sketch an outline of how media analysis has evolved historically in response to wider social and political changes and shifts in academic fashion.

Each trend has usually been modified or refined to reappear at a later date so that the picture has become increasingly complex (as have the media!).

Phase 1: mass society 1900–30s

Mass society theory flourished in the 1930s as part of a general theory of social change. The belief that the new urban areas were populated by a 'mass' of isolated individuals, rootless, alienated and deprived of face-to-face, primary group social relations, typical of the rural village, led many writers to speculate that such individuals were extremely vulnerable to the emergent forms of impersonal mass communication: the cinema and the radio. These fears were reinforced by the rise of the Nazi party in Germany, which appeared to be able to mobilise popular support through its effective use of the mass media as vehicles for its political propaganda. Thus the media were capable of mass manipulation.

Although relying almost entirely on unsupported speculation, this model of a powerful force exploiting an ignorant mass (sometimes known as the 'hypodermic needle' theory) has maintained a popular appeal among a variety of social and political commentators. We have been alerted to the dangers of insidious mass advertising preying on our unconscious mind, of the popular media creating illiteracy (see Fig. 1.3) and debasing cultural standards, of violence on our screens producing a nation of callous juvenile hooligans, and numerous other 'moral panics' within the framework of a mass manipulative model of the media. Television, in particular, has been singled out as all-powerful – TV controllers being referred to as the 'new priesthood' (with the decline of the Church's influence in society), and the world seen as reduced to a 'global village' via the means of the TV screen. Within sociological circles, however, support for the mass society theory declined after the Second World War due to a growing body of evidence which contradicted the theory's claims.

Phase 2: effects studies 1940s–60s

Once empirical research into measuring the actual effects which the media had on its audience was undertaken, it quickly became apparent that the audience was far from being a mass of isolated individuals but was, instead, made up of members of distinctive social groups. Within such groups 'opinion leaders' would interpret media messages on behalf of the rest of the group in a process which became known as the 'two step flow'.

Figure 1.3
TV-addict children 'lack concentration'
Morning television is reducing children's attention spans so they cannot concentrate at school, according to the head of Labour's new literacy task force. Michael Barber, a professor at London's Institute of Education, told head teachers yesterday that schools should advise parents to encourage their children to read more and watch television less.

He attacked Channel 4's *Big Breakfast* programme, saying it led to pupils arriving at school unprepared for lessons.

"Do we have to put up with the *Big Breakfast* or the moving wallpaper that passes for children's television?" he asked.

Although there is no reputable research on the effects of cartoons and other children's programmes on education, they might cause under-achievement in later life, he said.

Just as babies given dummies in the 1920s were found to do less well in later life, academics in 2050 might find that today's television had had a similar effect, he told the National Association of Head Teachers' conference in Torquay.

Mr Barber praised strong dramas, such as *Byker Grove*, a children's soap set in the north-east, and computer games which demanded participation rather than passive observation.

Television and games should excite the imagination and encourage young people to seek information about the world, he suggested.

While high-profile school discipline problems tended to capture headlines, children's inability to concentrate was a bigger issue for schools, he said. Parents, teachers and the media should work to ensure that children read more books and watched quality television.

"Television has many positive aspects but the problem is that children watch it to the exclusion of reading," he said.

Mr Barber said the real issue was to find ways of raising all pupils' reading ages to that of the current average by the age of 11, within 10 years. The most important factors would be raising teaching standards and encouraging effective parenting he said.

Mr Barber was a member of the Government's first education association, which was sent into Hackney Downs School in east London and which recommended its closure. Labour's Education spokesman, David Blunkett, appointed him this week to head a task force which will set targets for schools to raise standards of literacy.

Source: Fran Abrams, *The Independent*, 1 June 1996.

Also, social psychological research of media consumption showed that the audience both selected and filtered from what was available, rejecting messages which were not consonant with existing attitudes or beliefs, so that, in the long run, the media were simply reinforcing these attitudes and beliefs, not changing them. This, it was argued, helped to explain the impotence of the media to make any impact on the political opinions of the voters during election campaigns.

The uses and gratifications model of the media was a natural development from this effects research, focusing on what individual needs were supplied or gratified by a media industry anxious to maximise its audience rather than change them in any way. This shift towards a view of the media as largely in harmony with their audience is, to some degree, a reflection of the period in question. Functionalist accounts of consensus and social integration were dominant, and the Western nations (especially the USA) were experiencing unprecedented prosperity.

Phase 3: the media as ideology 1960s –

During the late 1960s, a series of social and political upheavals disrupted the prevailing stability and 'consensus'. Race riots in American cities, striking workers in western Europe and protesting anti-war students on both sides of the Atlantic helped to create a more critical academic atmosphere, not least in Marxist theory. As such, the media soon came under scrutiny and the conventional wisdom was challenged. The results and conclusions of effects studies were criticised on the grounds that the wrong questions were being asked about the media and their potential social influence. Could political effects be measured simply by looking at voting preferences and media use in an election campaign? What about the long-term cumulative political effects of daily news and current affairs coverage?

Of course, such long-term effects could never be empirically measured by interviewing audiences 'before' and 'after'. The whole process was too subtle and long term and, besides, both the media and the audience could not be isolated for research purposes from their social context, as some psychologists still attempt to do with television. Seen as a cultural product and part of a broader concern with the sociology of knowledge, media researchers began to look at media representations in terms of their ideological content, thus raising questions of power. The media have come to be recognised as crucial *cultural institutions* in which ideas and meanings are created and circulated within society.

Phase 4: texts, readers and popular culture 1970s –

The initial attraction in applying semiology to the study of the media was that it seemed to offer a much more systematic or scientific approach to discovering meanings. Each media text contained a structured language of sign systems, or codes, which could be broken down, or deconstructed, into its constituent parts in order to decode its meaning. Consequently, as ably demonstrated by the French writer Roland Barthes, any product of popular culture could be selected for the purposes of decoding.

While this may have shifted the emphasis away from discovering meanings from a media text's source (its 'author[s]'), it became an issue of debate as to how far meanings could be identified purely within the text or whether those who read the text (its audience) were ultimately the source of meaning. The 1980s saw a surge of sociological interest into how social groups differentially decoded the media according to gender, class, ethnicity, etc.

During the 1980s there a convergence of sociological and semiological/structuralist theories of the media, which formed the core for the foundation of media studies as an academic subject in its own right. As if to underline the growing cultural significance of the media, a parallel development was the emergence of a key theoretical concept, *postmodernism*.

A postmodern society is said to be one in which media images and signs become a primary source for shaping personal identities and our sense of social reality. This has echoes of earlier models of mass society theory particularly with respect to the growing trend towards a global culture in which media images such as Disney or Michael Jackson become universally recognised. However, postmodernist theorists also claim that media culture provides an everincreasing choice of images and identities. The media industries themselves are prone to blending and borrowing images from a range of past and present sources, a process known as *bricolage*, and, in turn, an increasingly media–literate audience is able to consume selectively from a vast media 'image bank' in pursuit of pleasure and identity. This is nowhere more apparent than in advertising.

Further examples of postmodernism are discussed on pages 45–47.

While postmodernism claims have some validity with respect to the phenomena of media saturation and intertextuality, its critics argue that its claims are exaggerated. Few people's lives are so built around media consumption that other sources of influence, such as family, education, etc., are negated. Furthermore, there is no real interrogation of the material production of media culture and whether or how inequalities of

Figure 1.4a

SUITS © HARVEY NICHOLS

Figure 1.4b

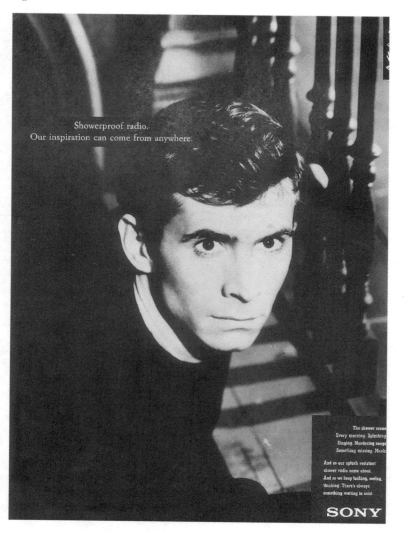

power are sustained. However bountiful and prevalent media images and signs are, we are not equally situated as 'consumers' able to 'purchase' our identities to order. For many, the struggle to achieve the basic needs of everyday life, such as housing and good health, are still the overwhelming priority of life.

2 Production

Cultural production

Television, films, magazines, etc., are all examples of cultural production. Unlike, say, a television set or compact disc player, which are both primarily material goods bought for a specific use, cultural products contain social meanings, ideas, knowledge, taste, etc. It is possible to look at *Gone with the Wind* as simply a film which has been consumed as an entertainment commodity by millions worldwide, or also as a meaningful film which says a lot about American attitudes towards its own history in the deep south. To take a second example, we might consider the song 'White Christmas'. On the one hand, the composer, Irving Berlin, may have been expressing a personal and emotional sentiment. On the other hand, his song may have been written to meet the requirements of the record company to which he was contracted, who could then market the song and make it one of the best selling, and hence profitable, songs of all time.

The media as industry

Many sociologists have described the media as an *industry*, producing cultural goods for mass consumption with one overriding motive: profit. In fact, the term 'culture industry' was used in the 1940s by members of the *Frankfurt School* of critical theory (a Marxist-influenced group) to refer to cultural products being mass produced in a manner no different from motor cars:

> 'for automobiles, there are such differences as the number of cylinders, cubic capacity, details of patented gadgets; for films there are the number of stars, the extravagant use of technology, labour and equipment, and the introduction of the latest psychological formulas' (Adorno and Horkheimer, in Curran et al., 1977)

Industrial production, with visions of mass manufacture of standardised goods in factory conditions, which are then sold in the market place to the public, seems a long way from the popular idea of the creativity and artistic endeavour which contribute to the cultural production of films, novels, music, etc. However, as Fred Inglis notes (see Fig. 2.1), cultural production does require almost constant innovation in a way that is not typical of other consumer products such as washing machines or breakfast cereals.

Figure 2.1

Capitalist production depends on the successful mass production and distribution of its commodity. The more sold, the lower the price can be dropped, the higher the marginal rate of profit and the more efficient the economies of scale. To regulate this process capitalist production typically builds in the deliberate tendency of the commodity to become obsolete. This cycle of purchase–obsolescence–replacement is standardly smoothed along by advertisements persuading consumers to replace what is still new. The cycle is the dynamo of capitalism. However, it is also important to that production that innovation is kept as cheap as possible. This year's car should be as like as possible to last year's car. New technology costs a lot. The research towards and development of a prototype is the most expensive stage of the productive sequence.

These necessities run solidly up against the demand of cultural activity that its material be freely chosen and, preferably, new. Of course a gradual selection of old favourites is chosen by the culture at different class levels and canonized as classics. The film, music and book industries are each immensely relieved when any work moves out of the dating process in this way and onto the timeless shelf of classics, since regular sales can then be assured for a long, safe time (especially if the classic becomes officially examinable, and appears in the syllabuses).

But, by and large, the first value of a cultural product is its novelty. If you watch people in a video-hire shop, they will put back the videotape they know they have seen, unless it's an old friend. The queue is longest for the latest thing. Cultural consumption resists in this way the drive of production towards stereotyping products. Each product – film, novel, music – resembles the development of a prototype.

Source: Fred Inglis, *Media Theory*, 1990.

How then do the different media operations resemble industrial production?

1 Film

Cinema as industrial production might be said to characterise Hollywood during the 1930s and 1940s. At the centre was the *studio system*. The major film companies, like MGM, Warner Brothers and United Artists, formed a monopolistic organisation, the Motion Picture Producers and Distributors of America, which effectively prevented any new competition. With strong support from the banks, the film companies owned the studios, distribution networks and cinema chains, and thus could ensure that their products were always available to the public. Following the control of the American market, they turned to foreign markets, where they quickly gained a dominating position, particularly as they were in a position to offer what was often a technically superior product at a lower price. Even today much of the film making in Europe is dependent upon American finance.

In terms of company assets, the phenomenon of *stars* was a vital aspect of Hollywood film economics. The studios had stars like Bette Davis, Clark Gable and Marilyn Monroe in contract, and could therefore be guaranteed so many of their films each year as a form of investment. Stars were especially important in marketing films. They promised audiences a particular and predictable form of pleasure. The history of Hollywood is full of stories of actors and actresses who tried unsuccessfully to break out of the stereotype which their 'star' image represented, the control of the industry to which they belonged being too great (see Fig. 2.2).

The industrial nature of film production could also be seen to shape the structure and content of the end product. The standardised form of storytelling, posing a problem at the beginning and resolving it at the end of the film, was commercially successful, and, therefore, opportunity for experimentation or variation was very limited.

Furthermore, films were classified or packaged according to their subject matter, style and conventions, in order to facilitate marketing and promotion to an audience who soon learned what to expect from such film types, or *genres*, such as musicals, horror films, westerns and gangsters. While many films do not easily fit such generic labels, any significant commercial success is likely to inspire sequels until audience demand falls away. Prominent examples include the *Jaws* and *Star Wars* cycles of films. Because of the large capital investment required for most Hollywood films, every effort is made to minimise the risk of losing money at the

Figure 2.2
The star system
From a business point of view, there are many advantages in the
star system. The star has tangible features which can be advertised
and marketed – a face, a body, a pair of legs, a voice, a certain
kind of personality, real or synthetic – and can be typed as the
wicked villain, the honest hero, the fatal siren, the sweet young
girl, the neurotic woman. The system provides a formula easy to
understand and has made the production of movies seem more
like just another business. The use of this formula may serve also
to protect executives from talent and having to pay too much
attention to such intangibles as the quality of a story or of acting.
Here is a standardised product which they can understand, which
can be advertised and sold, and which not only they, but also banks
and exhibitors, regard as insurance for large profits.
Source: Hortense Powdermaker, in her 'anthropological investigation'
of *Hollywood, The Dream Factory*, 1950.

box office. Perhaps the most calculating strategy is to film more than one
ending and test-market the different versions to discover the most
popular version prior to general release.

2 Television

Hollywood genre films still hold sway over modern audiences, if only
through the domestic medium of television. However, television has
evolved its own genre within the series format. Such examples include
situation comedy, soap opera and current affairs programmes. Series fit
very much into the industrial assembly line mode of production as they
allow for rationalised planning to produce a uniform end product. Stuart
Hood (1980) former controller of BBC television programmes, uses the
term 'regular strike' to refer to 'the production rhythm which can be
calculated and repeated with ease' (see Fig. 2.3).

Soap opera serials are a striking example of such continuous
production. The longevity of *Coronation Street* (1960) and *EastEnders*
(1985) has meant that a whole infrastructure could be built to sustain the
weekly episodes. This includes purpose-built sets (with its own guided

Figure 2.3   TV series as industralised production

The series form is the basic unit of calculation for TV production, and the basic unit of programme scheduling. Increasingly, all TV broadcast output has been scheduled according to the model of the series: even one-off plays of radically different aesthetic aspirations have been flung together to form a series: *The Wednesday Play, Play for Today, Second City First*. The series is equally the basic unit of marketing for broadcast TV. Single programmes are not usually advertised (unless special events like a Royal Wedding), but series are. Single episodes can be accounted failures where a series can be a success according to whatever criteria are used. The series is the formal equivalent to industrialised production: it represents the repetition of tasks at the level of programme format, narrative problematic, character and location. The scale of production implied by the series form requires that almost all tasks involved can be performed indiscriminately by anyone of the required grade, except for those acknowledged 'creative' functions which are confined to writer and performer.

Broadcast TV is geared to producing a series commodity consisting of a number (which may be huge, e.g. *Panorama*, news bulletins, etc.) of individual programmes which have a high degree of similarity. The production of these commodities is organised on industrial lines. The tasks involved are specified and personnel are organised into various grades responsible for a particular task or tasks. The tasks involved are standardised as much as possible to provide the maximum interchangeability of labour.

Source: J. Ellis, *Visible Fictions*, 1982.

tour in the case of *Coronation Street*), teams of scriptwriters working in rotation, and actors on long-term contracts.

Profit in commercial television is related to audience size, which means that if a programme is watched by millions of viewers then the ITV companies can sell advertising space at very high prices. Such is the growing pressure on such companies to achieve good audience ratings for programmes that new series need to prove instantly popular to justify continued investment and the commissioning of further series. In the case of continuous soap opera serials, their success has been exploited through additional weekly episodes being introduced, moving British television closer to the American practice of strip schedules whereby programmes are shown at the same time each day of the week.

3 Newspapers / magazines

There has been a slow decline in sales in the newspaper industry as the availability of other sources of news, especially television, has increased. Competition between the popular daily tabloid newspapers has become ever more intense. The success of *The Sun*, with its format of stories designed to entertain and provoke its readers, coupled with a visually bold style, has been instrumental in shaping the tabloid market. To give a competitive edge to sales, nearly all Britain's national newspapers in the 1990s have resorted to two sales strategies typical of consumer businesses – price cutting and free offers.

Both newspaper and magazine publishers have increasingly focused on targeting specific audiences, so called *niche marketing*, in order to entice advertising revenue, rather than relying on income from the cover price. If a newspaper or magazine has a clearly defined social profile for its readers, e.g. age or social class, then advertisers can be more confident of reaching their potential customers.

4 Music

The music industry is big business. In 1995, music sales in Britain exceeded £1 billion. Even though consumer loyalty is not as stable, music companies try to achieve a 'brand identity' through their artists who are often signed to long-term contracts and marketed globally. Artists like Phil Collins, Eric Clapton and George Michael can, individually, earn more than many medium size companies, and so qualify as very valuable company assets.

Market uncertainty

Despite all the efforts of media companies to predict and shape audience demand for their products, the popular appeal, and hence profitability, of films, music, television programmes, etc., is very upredictable. Less than 5 per cent of music released in the form of singles or albums gains chart success. Even when significant capital investment and market research are applied, there is no guarantee of success.

EastEnders has been a major success for BBC TV since coming on air in 1985, consistently being rated Britain's most popular television production after *Coronation Street*. However, when the BBC tried to repeat this soap opera success with £10 million investment and the

EastEnders producer, it proved a dramatic failure. *Eldorado* survived for only 12 months and never gained a significant audience size.

Perhaps the media industry with the greatest degree of uncertainty and potential financial risk is the cinema. The box office fate of some films can virtually make or break a production company and in the last 20 years a number of financial disasters have emanated from Hollywood. In 1980, *Heaven's Gate* lost $34.5 million, followed in 1982 by *Inchon* which lost $44 million. The star system, which used to guarantee a sizeable audience interest in films showcasing the most popular actors and actresses, no longer applies. Having said that, risks may be minimised if the right stars, whose global reputation will help to secure international sales, are cast within productions (See Fig. 2.4).

Media ownership – the Marxist case

Writing over a century ago, Karl Marx argued that, within a capitalist economy, the group with most power was the property–owning class, the bourgeoisie, whose primary interest was accruing more and more profit. This relationship between economic ownership and political power has been labelled *political economy*, and is seen by many as the key determining influence in shaping media output.

Marx himself predicted that successful capitalist enterprises would grow in size until a few companies would dominate the market. Modern Marxists have placed great emphasis on this trend, charting the progress of a small number of large corporations who now have a high degree of concentrated ownership in the media industries. With respect to the British media, this development was first outlined in detail by Murdock and Golding (1977) who noted that, because of a series of mergers and takeovers, by the beginning of the 1970s the top five companies accounted for between 70–80 per cent control of each media sector. Furthermore, they described the growth in interconnections between shareholders of different companies which formed a powerful web of cross-media interests which undermined genuine competition between companies.

Since the 1970s, there has been no reduction in the trend towards concentrated media ownership (see Fig. 2.5). Two processes can be seen to underpin the trend. Firstly, there is *horizontal integration*, whereby a media company takes over a smaller competitor in the same market, e.g. Thorn EMI's takeover of Virgin Records for £560 million in 1992. Secondly, there is *vertical integration*, whereby a media company acquires

Figure 2.4

Power trip Hollywood's most powerful actors (last year's ranking, where applicable, in brackets).	
1 Tom Hanks	(1)
2 Tom Cruise	(2)
3 Jim Carrey	(3)
4 Mel Gibson	(4)
5 Kevin Costner	(6)
6 Robin Williams	(11)
7 Brad Pitt	(16)
8 Harrison Ford	(5)
9 Clint Eastwood	(10)
10 Arnold Schwarzenegger	(7)
11 Robert Redford	(14)
12 Michael Douglas	(8)
13 Bruce Willis	(19)
14 Sylvester Stallone	(13)
15 Julia Roberts	(12)
16 John Travolta	(–)
17 Demi Moore	(9)
18 Jodie Foster	(17)
19 Sandra Bullock	(–)
20 Keanu Reeves	(18)
21 Sharon Stone	(22)
22 Whitney Houston	(–)
23 Michelle Pfeiffer	(–)
24 Denzel Washington	(23)
25 Robert de Niro	(–)
	Source: Premiere

The figures are based on box office takings and the ease with which a film can be made once the name is attached to it.

control of part of the production process at a different stage in the cycle. This has been particularly noticeable with electronics companies, like Sony, who manufacture the hardware, such as compact disc players or televisions, buying into software companies, like Columbia, who produce the music and programmes to 'feed' the hardware.

Figure 2.5   Share of the national voice

		national press	local press	TV	radio	total
1	Other media owners	1.3%	47.8%	16.0%	31.6%	23.2%
2	BBC	–	–	43.6%	50.3%	19.7%
3	News International	35.3%	–	1.9%	–	10.6%
4	Mirror Group	26.1%	–	0.5%	–	7.6%
5	Daily Mail & Gen. Trust	12.4%	14.3%	0.2%	0.9%	7.8%
6	United News and Media	14.4%	5.7%	–	–	5.7%
7	Carlton Communications	–	–	10.9%	–	3.1%
8	Thomson Newspapers	–	10.2%	–	–	2.9%
9	ITC	–	–	10.1%	–	2.9%
10	Granada Group	–	–	8.9%	–	2.5%
11	Pearson	1.0%	5.7%	1.5%	–	2.3%
12	Guardian Media Group	2.9%	3.6%	0.7%	–	2.0%
13	Daily Telegraph	6.6%	–	–	–	1.9%
14	Emap	–	3.7%	–	4.8%	1.7%
15	Trinity Holdings	–	6.0%	–	–	1.7%
16	Capital Radio	–	–	–	9.0%	1.3%
17	MAI	–	–	4.1%	–	1.2%
18	Reed Elsevier	–	3.0%	–	–	0.9%
19	GWR Group	–	–	–	3.4%	0.5%
20	DCI/Cox/TCI/Flextech	–	–	1.6%	–	0.5%

The British Media Industry Group devised "share of national voice" as a way of accounting for the influence of cross media ownership and of calculating the influence of the modern media companies. It is defined as any one company's overall share of the combined consumption of national and paid for regional papers, of radio listening and of TV viewing. The share of voice percentages combines figures from ABC, the Newspaper Society, Rajar and Barb. Because most of radio is music (and thus has less effect on diversity of view) radio listening figures are down-weighted by 50 per cent. The main criticism of the share of voice approach is that including the BBC and C4 underestimates the way the rest of Britain's media ownership is concentrated in so few private hands.

Source: Steve Peak, Paul Fisher, ed., *The Media Guide*, 1996.

This is not a new development. As early as the 1930s the British cinema industry was dominated by two vertically integrated companies – ABC and Rank. What is relatively new is the emergence of large media companies or *conglomerates* who have a significant share of several media markets simultaneously. What is more, these conglomerates tend to own media companies on an international scale. For a profile of one of the largest of these global media companies, News Corporation, see Fig. 2.6.

Figure 2.6 News Corporation Worldwide

Television

USA: Fox Broadcasting Company
        Fox Television
        Fox News

Australia: Seven Network (15%)

Cable and Satellite Television

USA: FX Network

UK: B Sky B (40%)

Australia: Foxtel (50%)

Asia: STAR TV
        ZEE TV (49.9%)

Latin America: News Corp/Glob (50%)
                Canal Fox

Germany: VOX (49.9%)

Filmed Entertainment

USA: Fox Filmed Entertainment
        incl. Twentieth Century Fox,
        Fox 2000, Fox Animation

Australia: Fox Studios

Newspapers

USA: *New York Post*

UK: *The Times*
      Sunday Times
      The Sun
      News of the World

Australia: *The Australian*
        plus 119 state and local
        newspaper titles

New Zealand: Independent
        Newspapers (50%)

Magazines

USA: *TV Guide*
        The Weekly Standard

UK: *Times Educational Supplement*
      TV Hits (45%)
      Inside Soap (45%)
      Sugar (45%)

Australia: *TV Hits* (45%)
        plus 14 other magazine titles

Other

USA: Harper Collins Book Publishing
        News Electronic Data
        Delphi Internet Services

UK: News Multimedia Ltd.
        Sky Radio (71%)

Source: The News Corporation Limited, *Annual Report 1995.*

One of the main advantages of such cross-media ownership is that individual media products may be extended into other media forms under the same company's umbrella. For example, a film may have a music soundtrack, a book, a magazine and television series, all produced as an accompaniment to the original story. This phenomenon, known as *multimarketing*, has been increasingly prevalent, especially where a large children's audience is involved, e.g. most of the recent Disney films like *Toy Story*, *The Lion King* and *Pocahontas*. Cross-media ownership also facilitates cross-media marketing. Rupert Murdoch's ownership of several newspapers like *The Sun* and *News of the World* has enabled him to promote B Sky B heavily to the readers of these newspapers (the very group most likely to invest in a satellite dish and subscribe to B Sky B).

The main concern of critics of this trend towards growing concentration of media ownership is that it represents a concentration of social and political power. In a much quoted passage in *The German Ideology*, Marx wrote that, 'The class which has the means of material production at its disposal has control at the same time over the production and distribution of the ideas of their age.' Very simply, the ruling class, the owners of the means of production, also owns, and therefore controls, the means of cultural production, including the media, which enables their ideas to become the ruling ideas of the day.

It is not easy to demonstrate a simple connection between economic and cultural power in contemporary society, but it is evident that owners of large media corporations do have the opportunity to significantly influence political decision making in a way which promotes their own economic interests. Rupert Murdoch has regularly intervened to determine which political party or candidate has the backing of his newspapers. In the case of Britain, *The Sun's* partisan support for the Conservative Party between 1979 and 1992 was undoubtedly a factor in boosting the number of its working class readers voting Tory. A more striking example is that of Silvio Berlusconi in Italy. In the 1994 Italian elections, he used his three television stations (with 40 per cent of the Italian audience) and other media interests to create popular support for his own, newly invented political grouping, Forza Italia, and his subsequent election as Italian President.

The pluralist critique

Writing from the perspective that power in society is not concentrated in the hands of any group, but is shared by a variety of competing interest groups, the pluralist approach tends to see the media as faithfully reflecting this diversity of interest.

There are several differences of opinion with the Marxist model, notably the following three points:

1 Not all the media organisations are constrained by the profit motive. The prime example here is *public service* broadcasting. The BBC is financed mainly by the public purchase of television licences, and is thus independent of the need to make a profit and satisfy shareholders. Instead, its remit is to provide a range of programmes that includes something to satisfy all viewers regardless of income. In addition, all licenced broadcasting organisations in Britain are required to be politically impartial, thus preventing a government or powerful interest using television and radio for its own political purposes.

2 *Minority interests* are served by the media. This is facilitated both via public service broadcasting (especially through Channel 4 which is committed to meeting the needs of groups like ethnic minorities) and commercial media companies. There has been a growth of niche targeting of distinctive audience interest groups as evidenced by the massive expansion of magazine titles available in Britain in the last decade. There are, for example, over 50 computer-related magazines published each month. Furthermore, some of these products contain content critical of powerful groups in society, e.g. socialist or environmental publications. Music which could be described as anti-authoritarian or political has appeared on labels attached to major music companies, e.g. hardcore rap in the USA during the early 1990s. This leads on to a third point.

3 *Supply meets demand*, i.e. ultimate control rests with the consumer; a point often strongly voiced by owners and controllers within media organisations, summed up in the notion that 'we are giving the public what they want'. Any other interpretation would be a case of overestimating the power of the media companies to dictate what their audiences wanted.

The Marxist reply: the influence of profit

While the pluralist critique has shaken the Marxist case in the eyes of many media sociologists, the following points of defence have been made by the Marxists in relation to each of the three main criticisms mentioned above.

1   Public broadcasting cannot stand outside of the economic pressures which affect the commercial TV companies who need to attract advertisers by winning large audiences. Prior to 1955, the BBC enjoyed a monopoly position in broadcasting and so was not overly concerned with the size of its audience. With the introduction of competition from ITV, the BBC no longer felt secure about its support from licence fee revenue which was set by the government. It has been unofficially recognised by the BBC that, should its share of the national audience fall much below 30 per cent, then the licence fee would be hard to justify. During the 1990s, it has become increasingly managed as a commercial organisation with an aggressive search for audience ratings, which almost mirrors that of ITV.

2   Some minorities are catered for more than others. This point is argued on the basis that the profitability of media products depends on either circulation/sales or advertising revenue. In the case of smaller audiences, if they have above average purchasing power then advertisers are keen to reach them.

Such influence is particularly evident with the commercial viability of newspapers and magazines. For example, the combined daily sales of the five British upmarket broadsheet newspapers (*The Times, The Guardian, Daily Telegraph, Financial Times* and *Independent*) averages approximately 2 ½ million, while the five middle and downmarket tabloid daily newspapers (*The Sun, Daily Mirror, Daily Star, Daily Mail* and *Daily Express*) average 11+ million. Meanwhile, working class papers like the *News Chronicle* and the *Daily Herald*, each with over a million readers, have folded (see Fig. 2.7).

Women's magazines show not only a bias towards the interests of middle class readers, but also to women aged from 16 to 34, the age group whose spending power makes them most attractive to advertisers.

3   The pluralist emphasis on the power of the consumer in shaping media markets is seen as a gross exaggeration. Apart from the bias towards the more affluent social groups, the media companies are seen as being conservative and reluctant to experiment with new formats or content despite evidence that so called 'minority' tasters are often discovered to have a mass audience appeal, whether it be televised snooker (the 1985 World Championship Final being watched by over 12 million after midnight) or the early films of Quentin Tarantino, e.g. *Pulp Fiction*, with their unusual narrative form and dark humour.

Furthermore, when new competition emerges, the large media corporations often try to use their superior financial power to squeeze

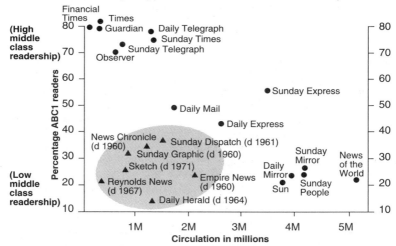

Figure 2.7   The Bermuda Triangle and the death of national newspapers`

("the last reported position of those national newspapers that have sunk since 1955, as well as the current (1977) plots of the survivors". Michael Mander)

Note: The seven national newspapers which died between 1960 and 1971 - four of them in 1960-1 - are shown in the circle of lowish circulation and low percentage of ABC1 readers. The survivors were all higher on circulation and/or ABC1 percentage.

Source: Michael Mander. 'The Intergration of advertising and circulation sales policies', J. Tunstall, 1983.

potential rivals through aggressive strategies such as price cutting or increased marketing. Between 1993 and 1995, Rupert Murdoch's News Corporation embarked on a price cutting war in the newspaper market in order to destabilise its main competitors who did not share the same ability to withstand the financial losses incurred by such price cuts (for example, *The Times* dropped its cover price from 45p to 20p which meant a loss of about 2p for every copy printed).

Ownership versus control

An important distinction to make concerning the management and control of modern business organisations is that between owners of companies, who possess the shares issued to raise capital, and employed managers, who rarely have any property rights concerning the company. This distinction is sometimes referred to as *allocative* control – the control over the amount of resources that are made available – and *operational* control – the day-to-day management and application of specialist knowledge as applied to the flow of media production.

Professionalism

Within media occupational groups, professionalism is where the skills and expertise of the occupation are valued as an ideal to which those in the profession should aspire. The particular craft or specialist ability required varies between different media professions, but the importance of such values lies in the way that the claim to professionalism is a means of retaining or negotiating some autonomy within media organisations. In other words, it is a justification for the film director, journalist, actor, etc., resisting 'outside' control, whether from the management, government or the public, and proceeding according to their own standards.

Within television, **Tom Burns** (1977), on the basis of 300 interviews with BBC staff, found that the *cult of professionalism* was one of the ways that programme makers were able to come to terms with the distance between themselves and the public whom they are supposed to serve. Another response was to hold to the longstanding Reithian view of 'public service', or simply a 'responsible attitude', while a third response was to make limited use of audience ratings as a gauge to their success. Burns found that the three different attitudes were often in conflict, with the newer 'professional' approach tending to undermine the traditional public service attitude through a mixture of referring to fellow professional standards and audience ratings as a way of judging the merit of a programme. Outside pressures, be they political or economic, were considered the problem of senior management.

Jeremy Tunstall's research (McQuail, 1972) into 207 specialist newsgathering journalists, through observation and unstructured interviews, showed that, in contrast to the audience and advertising revenue goals of news organisations, newsgathering journalists tended to emphasise a 'non-revenue goal'. Some, like foreign correspondents, were relatively free to produce their stories, while others, like crime reporters, were expected to keep in mind the need for maximum readership. Autonomy could be achieved by negotiation, for example, by the need to keep a source confidential, as with political correspondents whose need to protect their close links with politicians can be used to justify the way they present a story.

Other studies of journalists have made the distinction between straight reporters, gathering news through recognised channels, and committed 'investigative' reporters, campaigning on issues or causes (perhaps the most celebrated example being the Watergate journalists, Woodward and Bernstein, on the *Washington Post*, who negotiated the freedom to pursue the exposure of corruption in the White House). On television, institutional space has been given to this style of journalism in programmes, like *World in Action*, which are often critical of powerful interest groups.

Another strategy for achieving some autonomy within media production is the emphasis on *cultural creativity*. Artistic merit is acknowledged and rewarded in most areas of media production, e.g. The American Film Academy Awards (the 'Oscars'), the BPI music awards (the 'Brits'), etc. With respect to cinema, a number of film directors, such as John Ford, Orson Welles and Martin Scorsese, have been credited with bringing to their films a personal artistic vision and style (the *auteur* concept). The ensuing reputation can provide some protection from the institutional constraints experienced by less exalted film directors.

The constraints on professional autonomy

There seems to be a good argument to be made for the influence of the autonomous professional working within the media. However, this can be easily exaggerated.

1 Institutional organisation

Little media production emanates from individuals working independently in isolation. Rather, the situation usually involves a high degree of mutual cooperation and interdependence in which production decisions are dependent upon consultation and compromise as described by Stuart Hood with respect to the BBC (see Fig. 2.8). Furthermore, as with any organisation, there is normally a hierarchical structure in which the key decisions are taken by those in positions of seniority. For example, in the production of a newspaper, the choice of lead story for the front page (the 'splash') is usually taken by the editor. Reporters writing stories for inclusion in the paper may find their contribution is ignored ('spiked') or drastically edited to give it a different angle by those further down the production chain, the sub editors.

Figure 2.8   Occupational Socialisation

What is common to both BBC and the commercial television companies, however, is the process of learning the rules of the institution, which begins as soon as anyone is appointed to their staff. This process is mainly an informal one and is at work in any large organisation. It is true that in the case of the BBC there are in-house training courses, which are a formal part of the process of moulding staff so that they will function well and efficiently within the limits set by the organisation; but as in other organisations much of what the newcomers learn is picked up from colleagues at work, in the canteen or in the pub favoured by their associates. They may learn that a story or programme idea which they consider 'interesting' is not so, that certain people are not suitable subjects for interview, or that certain words to describe persons or events are 'inappropriate', that a particular piece of film is not suitable for inclusion in a programme or only in certain circumstances or in certain contexts . . .

To information acquired in the day-to-day contacts of work and leisure must be added the contents of the directives which filter down through large organisations from policy meetings. These are gatherings of senior executives at which gate-keeping in the grand manner goes on, where – in the news departments, for instance – decisions are taken as to which events should be covered by film or television cameras, where it is laid down what names should be applied to groups or individuals and who shall be allowed access to the microphone or television camera. Membership of such policy-making committees is restricted but there are departmental meetings at which the directives emanating from the policy-makers are passed on, discussed and interpreted. By participating at meetings at departmental level newcomers learn how the organisation works, what policies it pursues, what degree of latitude is possible within the bounds of policy. They learn here and by experience in what directions the organisation is prepared to be liberal and what directions it is not. They will become aware over a period of time of changes in policy and discover that within the organisation there are different tendencies, for even an organisation like the BBC is not monolithic; it can accommodate what are seen – in organisational terms – as progressives and conservatives . . .

But above all they must learn the limits of the possible – the limits set by the management of the BBC, by the management of the television companies and by their supervisory body, the Independent Broadcasting Authority.

Source: Hood, 1980.

2 Intervention by the owners

Although owners of media companies rarely have the specialist knowledge or opportunity to interfere directly during the production process, they can exert influence over the content for other than simply commercial reasons. Probably the most notorious examples are to be found in the newspaper industry where individual owners have frequently used their newspapers as a form of political or social 'mouthpiece' for their views. Robert Maxwell regularly generated or even personally wrote stories concerning issues he felt were important (including his own life story!) during his tenure as the *Daily Mirror's* proprietor in the 1980s. Rupert Murdoch has frequently ensured that his newspapers support the political parties or candidates most likely to benefit his business interests. In Murdoch's case his own journalistic experience has enabled him to exercise a 'hands-on' interference in the choice and treatment of stories in his newspapers.

Few editors are in a position actively to resist or contradict their owners' wishes, regardless of their own journalistic reputation. The highly respected editor Harold Evans soon resigned from *The Times* after Rupert Murdoch acquired the newspaper in 1981. Curran and Seaton (1991) claim there has been only one instance when the unity of journalists on a British newspaper successfully defied their owner. The occasion (in 1984) was when Donald Trelford, the editor of *The Observer*, refused to withdraw a story which was critical of the political regime in Zimbabwe, a country in which *The Observer's* owner, Tiny Rowland, had significant business investments. Nevertheless, it seemed that many subsequent stories relating to Tiny Rowland were biased in favour of his company.

3 Regulatory constraints

No media production can ignore the existence of a range of rules and regulations which restrict what can be represented in public. Various laws have been enacted which apply across all the media.

These have a number of objectives including:

1 the protection of national security, e.g. The Official Secrets Act
2 the protection of audiences from potentially corrupting or offensive influences, e.g. The Obscene Publications Act
3 the protection of individuals from being unjustly represented in a harmful way – the laws against libel
4 the protection of the Christian religion from outrageous comments or ridicule – the laws against blasphemy.

In addition, each media institution has its own specific legislation, such as the various Broadcast Acts which have controlled the issue of licences to broadcast as well as establishing the principles of public service and political impartiality. To administer these regulations and guidelines, a range of institutional bodies have been established.

The main ones are:

1 Independent Television Commission
2 Radio Authority
3 Broadcasting Standards Commission
4 Advertising Standards Authority
5 British Boards of Film and Video Classification
6 Press Complaints Commission.

One important implication of all this regulatory constraint on media freedom is that it provides a significant potential for governmental influence on media production. Nowhere is this more controversial than in the politics of broadcasting where there has been a growing tension between the media professionals, striving to retain their independence, and politicians eager to manage their public image.

Finally, with respect to the issue of ownership and production, it is important to note that, apart from the longstanding anti-monopoly legislation which is designed to prevent excessive market domination by one or two companies, new rules have recently been introduced to address cross-media ownership. Mergers or takeovers involving companies from different media sectors will only be permitted providing there will still be diversity and 'proper competition'. In practice, this means setting maximum percentage shares for any one company within its own sector (e.g. an ITV company can only own franchises which cover a maximum 15% total television audience) and also other media sectors into which it might invest (e.g. a national newspaper company can buy only up to 15 per cent of the total television market). To strengthen these principles, it is proposed that, in the longer term, percentage limits will be set for the total media market share allowed for any one company (say, 10 per cent). However, this may be very difficult to measure in practice – would it be based on circulation and audience size, or revenue?

4 Economic constraints

Whatever autonomy can be negotiated by media professionals, the pressure on them to achieve commercial success is invariably an everpresent factor. Few working in the media are not conscious of the need to maximise audiences and minimise costs. Shareholders of private companies expect to benefit from an annual increase in profits and, notwithstanding artistic recognition, most of the awards and rewards go to those whose work generates the biggest audiences and the largest product units consumed. Even in publicly controlled organisations, such as the BBC, there has been a clear shift in the 1990s towards an entrepreneurial and accountancy culture which mirrors that of commercial broadcasting as they have striven, under their Director General, John Birt, to demonstrate that they give the public value for money.

As Marxist writers have continued to point out, the economic logic of capitalism is still a strong force in determining media production. However, as the above discussion has shown, it would be a mistake to see the imperative for profit as the *sole* determinant. This can be further demonstrated in considering the last theme of this chapter, independent media production.

Independent production

There is no one definition of what is meant by independent production, but in general terms it implies a freedom from some kind of external control, particularly economic or political. In practice this means not being answerable to a large business company or state-controlled institution.

Three features may apply in attempting to identify what is distinctive about independent production.

1 The organisation of production is more democratic or collectivist in nature. The participatory ethos may even extend to the audience

being able to make a genuine contribution. The classic example is the *fanzine* which literally means a magazine made by and for fans of a particular sub culture, be it football, rap music or science fiction films. Other examples based on collectivist production include community radio and newspaper, and film and video co-operative workshops.

2 Minority audiences are often the main target of independent producers. These might include ethnic, political, gay/lesbian and other groups whose culture and interests are often ignored by the mainstream media. Such groups may feel socially marginalised and a media voice is a significant means of cultural expression. This often includes a political agenda which contradicts or challenges the dominant or 'official' perspective found in the mainstream media. For example, *The Voice* is a newspaper which articulates a black point of view which is usually absent from the (white) national press. (See also Fig. 2.9 for a description of the role of football fanzines.)

3 Independent media production is often associated with innovatory style and design. Because its practitioners are either consciously rejecting the conservatism of the dominant media, or simply approaching media production with a more naive, do it yourself spirit, the 'rules' are happily broken or ignored. Consequently, independent media production is sometimes equated with *alternative* media production. New musical styles, such as hip hop (and later trip hop), rap and techno, regularly emerge from independent music labels before being recognised and embraced by the major music companies. Many of the audio–visual techniques found in television advertising or pop videos originated from experimental independent video production.

Figure 2.9
Football fanzines have been described as funny, irreverent and innovative . . .

Without exception they are born from a genuine love for the game and are fiercely loyal to it. Their concern lies not with their own individual interests but for the game as a whole. Collectively, they have become a movement, campaigning for a better deal for football fans, attempting to redress the overwhelming negative image in which both football and football fans are too often portrayed, while at the same time injecting their own brand of humour into the game – ranging from the gently mocking through to the bitingly cruel, and yet merely proving the old adage that it is only possible effectively to parody that which you hold in great affection.

Often scathing, disdainful and contemptuous towards those they see as exploiting football in a variety of ways, and dismissive, intolerant and sceptical of those they see as interfering in, and with, the game for a variety of reasons, their criticisms are almost always constructive, reasoned and articulate. Their existence puts paid to the stereo-typed image of the average football fan as being a moronic thug who can barely grunt, let alone put more than three words together. And their popularity is such that in only two seasons the number of titles available has leapt from less than a dozen to over two hundred . . .

It has also been suggested that the football fanzine is the written equivalent of the after-match conversation in the pub . . .

Another important reason for the popularity of fanzines is that they provide a forum for the views and opinions of football fans who hitherto had had no other outlet to air those views. This particularly applies to the 'political' issues, especially those that apply to an individual club and which are almost always suppressed within its official publications.

But it's not just the 'issues' which are openly debated within fanzines. Criticism and praise of the managers, players and playing styles are also aired . . .

Collectively, fanzines tread pretty much the ssame path, airing the same grievances, challenging the same issues, but at the same time they establish their own individual characteristics and style.

Source: Quentin Rogers, 'About Fanzines' in *The Best of the Football Fanzines*, 1990.

3 Representations

Mediated reality

Whatever the intentions of media producers, all forms of representation that are made available to audiences involve *mediation*. That is to say, social reality is transformed by the act of constructing a representation of that reality. Technically, no media form can physically deliver a pure experience of the world simply because it is being channelled or mediated through pictures, sounds and words (despite claims made for new technologies delivering 'virtual reality'). Such technological mediation alters the live experience of 'being there' and being able to observe and feel the scene directly.

Even more significantly, there is also social mediation arising from the choices made by media producers. This encompasses everything from selecting what subject to cover, to how it should be treated and presented to the audience. This assumes that there is an intention to reflect social reality faithfully in the first place. While news coverage and television genres such as documentary may set out to report on real events, much of media production is engaged with fiction and fantasy. It remains the case that all media texts contain representation of the world, be it a Disney cartoon or a television soap opera. The question remains, what kinds of representation are made available and, in particular, do they adequately reflect the diversity of interests and identities within society? Any attempt to answer this question must be rooted in a broader theoretical model of how media content is shaped and its function as a form of cultural communication.

Pluralist theory

The pluralist theory of power proposes that Western industrial societies are essentially democratic. No one group or élite dominates the rest of society and the balance of power is maintained by the state, the neutral institution of government. Pluralists see the media as being part of that democratic process whereby all points of view and interests are represented within the range of media output. This is seen to spring mainly from the workings of the free market of supply and demand (the *laissez-faire* model) discussed in Chapter 2. For example, the choice of women's magazines reflects the range of women's interests, from feminine to feminist.

Critical theories

There is a range of sociological/cultural theories which have addressed the issue of what kind of social reality is represented within the media. Pre-war *mass society* theories suggested that the media formed a vital aspect of élite control over the masses, e.g. Nazi propaganda. Contemporary examples might include states with a strong authoritarian central control, such as China or Saudi Arabia.

Within Marxism there has been a similar tradition of the 'conspiracy theory', based on a simple idea that the economic base of society determines the superstructure, i.e. the ruling economic class maintains its position of power through its control of social and political institutions including government and the media. Many of the cruder Marxist accounts of the media have emphasised their 'bias' or *'distortion' of social reality*, suggesting the media's role to be one of a mouthpiece for the ruling class. An often-cited example is the stand taken by the BBC during the General Strike of 1926. Lord Reith, the Director General of the BBC, wrote to Baldwin, the Prime Minister, during the strike that, 'Assuming the BBC is for the people, and that the Government is for the people, it follows that the BBC must be for the Government in this crisis too.' (Many critics of the media argued that a similar pro-government line was evident in 1984/5 during the miners' strike.) Thus, instead of the media reflecting the whole array of social and political interests, as suggested by pluralist accounts, one group, a ruling élite or class, is able to control the media and shape its content in order to protect its interests.

Few media sociologists (including Marxists) today adhere to either of these two approaches. In the 'new' sociology of the media, much work has gone into exposing the myth of the 'window on the world' notion of the media, but the analyses have stopped well short of any simple conspiracy theory. Instead, the question has arisen as to *how* and *to what extent* do the media serve the interests of the more powerful groups in society?

Ideology

In *The German Ideology* Marx wrote that the owners of the means of production, the ruling class, also control the production and distribution of ideas. Thus the ruling economic class is able to rule not by force but through ideas. These ideas function to protect ruling class interests by representing as natural the class relationships of production. For example, under feudalism, a dominant religious idea was that the social order was ordained by God (e.g. the divine right of kings to rule). Under capitalism, ruling class ideology would be found throughout the institutions of family, religion, government, etc., which comprise the 'superstructure' of society. The ideas and social relationships of the 'superstructure' legitimate the economic class relations of production, i.e. the 'base' of society.

Thus, in politics, a belief that government represents the 'national interest' (rather than ruling class interests as Marx believed) is ideological. Ideology, then, is a way of making sense of the world which produces a false consciousness of that world and so the reality of class domination and exploitation is not recognised. (By using the term *'false consciousness'*, Marx was intimating that a true or scientific consciousness was possible. Many neo-Marxist writers have argued that all consciousness is to some extent ideological as language can never be neutral.) Therefore, to refer to ideology is to suggest that meanings, beliefs and practices support particular group interests in society and are not natural or inevitable.

How is ideological domination achieved?

Marx did not make this explicit in his writings and so Marxist writers have had to develop a fuller explanation. This has become essential given that the proletariat have showed less and less evidence of becoming class-conscious and overthrowing capitalism. It is not surprising then that the media should have increasingly come under critical scrutiny by neo-Marxist writers. Some consider it to be the most significant part of the superstructure of advanced capitalist societies. However, the various schools of Marxist thought have been unable to agree on exactly how class domination is achieved through the media. The problem of 'proving' that the media are, in fact, an instrument of class control has led to debates between Marxists, as well as criticisms by other sociological perspectives, notably pluralism.

Among the main Marxist contributions to the sociology of the media have been the following:

1 The Frankfurt School

They were among the first to suggest that capitalist control of the mass media was the main reason why capitalism had survived and flourished in the post-war period. Herbert Marcuse (1964) argued that the media helped 'indoctrinate and manipulate, they promote a false consciousness which is immune against its falsehood'. He further claimed that the media deprived art of any critical value by reducing it to mere commerce, e.g. Watney's took the Communist slogan 'Red Revolution' and used it in an advertising campaign to promote sales of their 'Red Barrel' beer. Marcuse and others of the Frankfurt School have been criticised for adopting an élitist view of mass (rather than class) society, in which all popular culture is dismissed as 'mass deception', a rather determinist view.

2 Economic determinism

In Chapter 2, we saw how Murdock and Golding (1977) charted the increasing concentration of capitalist ownership of the media. Here the emphasis is very much on the economic base of society determining the media as part of the superstructure. Again, critics have asked, does it automatically follow that this produces a particular ideological effect? The owners, with economic, allocative control, are separate from the media professionals, who have day-to-day operational control, and there is little evidence that the owners directly intervene in such operational control. This view has been criticised for being over-determinist.

3 Althusser

The French Marxist, Althusser, used the term 'ideological state apparatus' to refer to the social institutions, including the media, that reproduce ideology in a way that represents capitalism as natural and inevitable. In order to fulfil this function they must be *relatively autonomous* from the direct control of the ruling class, i.e. they must be seen to be independent and self-governing. The fact that TV news is seen as objective and neutral would fit this idea of 'relative autonomy'. Otherwise, the media would not be able to function ideologically and would be seen as 'biased'.

Althusser's work signalled a move away from looking at the economic determinants of the media to concentrate on how the media give ideological meaning to the world. In particular, Althusser was concerned with how they helped to create an imaginary picture of the real conditions of capitalist production for the subject, i.e. the audience, thus concealing the reality of exploitation. This is achieved by the media offering to subjects positions in which they (mis)recognise themselves – as free thinking individuals, members of a democratic society, discriminating consumers, etc.

4 Gramsci

The Italian Marxist, Gramsci's, use of the term *hegemony* has also been influential on Marxist media writers. This refers to the ability of the ruling class to rule by consent, rather than by force, over the working class. This is mainly achieved culturally through education, the media, etc. The media have a central role in producing a 'common sense', which is really a form of ideology. Like Althusser, Gramsci argued for the relative autonomy of the media, and took this further to suggest that the dominant class could never be sure of hegemonic order but, rather, it had to be struggled for against opposition, especially when capitalism passed through one of its periodic crises (e.g. an economic depression).

Consequently, there would need to be some accommodation of opposing groups' interests in order to protect ruling class ascendancy. Popular culture, including media production, can thus be seen as simultaneously containing dominant, subordinate and even oppositional ideological positions.

Whilst Gramsci related hegemony to class control, the recognition that there may be a range of competing ideologies circulating within popular culture provides an opportunity to consider other forms of power struggle that are not purely based on economic class. Perhaps the most prominent of these are struggles based on inequalities of gender, generation and race/ethnicity. Therefore, media culture allows space for the production of meanings, which is not straightforwardly determined by reference to the power of the capitalist class or any dominant group (see Fig. 3.1).

Figure 3.1

... hegemony theory allows us to think [of] popular culture as a 'negotiated' mix of intentions and counter-intentions: both from 'above' and from 'below', both 'commercial' and 'authentic'; a shifting balance of forces between resistance and incorporation. An interesting example is the reggae music of Rastafarian culture: Bob Marley had international success with songs articulating the values and beliefs of Rastafari. This success can be viewed in two ways. On the one hand, it signals the expression of the message of his religious convictions to an enormous audience worldwide; undoubtedly for many of his audience the music had the effect of enlightenment, understanding and perhaps even conversion to, and bonding for those already convinced of, the principles of the faith. On the other hand, the music made enormous profits for the music industry, promoters, Island Records, etc. What we have is a paradox in which the anti-capitalist politics of Rastafari are being 'articulated' in the economic interests of capitalism: the music is lubricating the very system it seeks to condemn. Yet it is still true that the music is an expression of an oppositional (religious) politics, and that this politics has certain political and cultural effects. But it is also true that the politics of Rastafari are expressed in a form which is ultimately of financial benefit to the dominant culture (i.e. as a commodity which circulates for profit). Therefore, Rastafarian reggae is a force for change which paradoxically stabilizes (at least economically) the actual power-base of the status quo.

Source: John Storey, *An Introductory Guide to Cultural Theory and Popular Culture*, 1993.

Relativist theories

As analyses of media culture have moved away from asserting a simple or close relationship between the meanings of media representations and their social structural determinants, more emphasis has been placed on the variety of interpretations and pleasures made available to modern media audiences. The premise that there are no fixed or absolute cultural meanings shared by social subjects has a long tradition within sociology in what is often referred to as the interpretivist tradition. An example of this is discussed below in relation to media labelling of deviance.

Semiology opened up the whole question of the range of meanings made possible in media forms of communication (or media *language*). Semiology (or semiotics) refers to the study of the meaning of signs. It derives from linguistics and attempts to understand how language, as a system of signs or code, communicates meaning. Language and other forms of communication are structured according to certain rules which are understood culturally (hence being literate means understanding those rules). What interests semiologists and, indeed, sociologists is the way that signs (like words or images) help us to make sense of the world, how they *signify reality*.

Roland Barthes, a French semiologist, distinguished between the way signs denote and connote meaning. *Denotation* refers to the simple and obvious meaning of a sign, e.g. a photograph of a street denotes that street. However, photographs are not simply a mechanical reproduction of reality. There is a process of human intervention in selecting how to photograph a street. This includes whether to use black and white or colour film, focus sharply or softly, etc. Black and white film, for example, may give the impression that it is an old photograph, or may make the street seem bleak. Barthes calls this *connotation*, the cultural meaning inferred in the sign. It is not fixed but is open to interpretation. A red flag could connote danger or Communism.

Through convention and use it has become symbolic of these ideas. *Myth* is the term Barthes uses to refer to a chain of ideas associated with a sign. By myth he doesn't mean they are false but that they represent cultural ways of making sense of the world. A picture of a white man wearing a white lab coat and standing next to a statistical diagram symbolises science – objective, factual (and white/masculine) knowledge – whereas a picture of a black man in exotic garments standing next to a large pot of boiling water over a fire symbolises primitiveness or even sorcery and witchcraft. These are cultural codes which we use to give meaning to the world, and which can be seen as ideological, the above being examples of both racist and sexist ideology.

In a novel, words (signs) are organised and structured to signify meaning within the text. Similarly, media texts contain sign systems or audio-visual codes which can be *decoded* to reveal the underlying ideology. When certain codes become popularly recognised, they are referred to as *genres*. These include such cinematic forms as the 'musical', the 'gangster movie', and the 'western'. We recognise the western by certain visual signs like the cowboys' clothes, the landscape, etc., and by narrative themes of the hunt for the outlaw, civilising the west, etc. The western's ideological messages concern American history – the American Indian as savage and aggressive, the triumph of law and order, etc. Genres, then, may carry certain meanings which limit how a given text can be interpreted. We may find it difficult to make sense of a dramatic political speech in the context of a situation comedy, other than as a send-up of politics.

What has made interpreting (or reading) media texts more complex is the tendency within the media to cross-reference, recycle and parody other media texts, a process which is often identified as belonging to *postmodernism*.

Postmodern texts are characterised by a number of features (although there is no consensus as to what the defining elements are). Among those features most often cited are, firstly, a breakdown in the distinction between art and popular culture as crossovers between the two increase. An example of this is the case of operatic music (Verdi's 'Nessun Dorma') as soundtrack for television coverage of the 1990 World Cup.

Secondly, postmodern texts tend to lack a clear sense of time and space, as exemplified by the film *Blade Runner* (see Fig. 3.2). With the growth in number of media sources, e.g. the dozens of television channels, and their global spread, it is claimed that our sense of historical time and geographical location have become easily confused.

Finally, the postmodern media are typified by a tendency playfully to expose and parody their own processes of production. This can be seen as a form of *deconstruction* in so far as it reveals the artifice of media texts. It is evident in much of contemporary television where genres such as talk shows have been subject to pastiche productions, e.g. *Knowing Me, Knowing You*. Production crews now actively participate in live television shows and even party election broadcasts have succumbed to the trend. In 1996, a Conservative Party election broadcast featured John Major, the Prime Minister, being filmed as he addressed another camera reading the script on an autocue.

Theory and method

The more that media texts are perceived as containing a multiplicity of potential meanings, the greater the difficulty there is in establishing patterns of representations and the exercise of ideological power. At its most relativist, the interpretive position negates such an approach and relegates any analysis of textual meanings to audience research (discussed

Figure 3.2

Figure 3.2
A frequently cited example of the postmodern film is *Blade Runner*
(1982). Amongst the more noticeable characteristics of this film
(which is about Los Angeles in the early part of the twenty-first
century), we can note how its architectural look, or production
design, clearly mixes styles from different periods. The buildings
which house the major corporation have lighting characteristic of
contemporary skyscrapers but the overall look of ancient temples,
while the 'street talk' consists of words and phrases taken from a
whole range of distinct languages. These architectural and
linguistic confusions can be said to contribute to an elusive sense
of time since we appear to be in the past, the present and the future
at the same time. It is a science fiction film which is not obviously
futuristic in its design. This effect is accentuated in two ways. First,
the 'non-human humans' in the film are not mechanical robots but
'replicants', almost perfect simulations of human beings. Second,
the genre of the film is not clear. It has been defined as a science
fiction film, but it is also a detective film. Its story unfolds as a
detective story, the hero has many of the character traits we
associate with the 'tough-guy' policeman or private investigator,
and his voice-over, which relates the investigation, draws upon the
idioms and tone of *film noir*.
    Source: Dominic Strinati, *An Introduction to Theories of Popular Culture*,
1995.

in Chapter 4). If we assume media texts can be scrutinised without
necessarily resorting to continuous audience confirmation then what
methods are available?

1 Content analysis

This involves the systematic counting and description of a large area of
media content. The researcher identifies a set of categories and then sets
out to record the frequency with which each category occurs within a
given area of the media. For a description of a typical example, see Fig.
3.3. Supporters of content analysis claim it to be objective because, firstly,
it is based on hard empirical data whose reliability can be checked and

Figure 3.3
Ten constituencies were chosen according to four political criteria:
the marginality of the particular contest, the incumbency status of
candidates, their party affiliation and their seniority within their
party and/or their national 'celebrity' status. These were identified
as factors which might be influential in attracting media interest in
the constituency.

A content analysis was conducted of the weekly paid-for, free
and daily newspapers circulating in the selected constituencies for
the 3 1/2 weeks of the election campaign. Each of the 1,194
election–related items published (921 articles, 35 editorials and 238
letters) was coded for thirty–eight variables – including
partisanship in reporting, status and party affiliation of candidates,
subject focus of the item (candidate, national policy or local issues),
the type of newspaper (weekly, daily, free), its structure of
ownership, whether private or chain, the position of the item in
the paper, the use of photographs and headlines and the week of
the campaign – to assess developments in the quantity and
direction of press reporting as the campaigning progressed.

NUMBER OF NEGATIVE AND POSITIVE APPRAISALS OF
PARTIES ACCORDING TO ITEM TYPE

	Conservative Party		Labour Party		Alliance	
	Positive	Negative	Positive	Negative	Positive	Negative
Article	177	251	150	230	94	81
Editorial	9	6	0	27	0	6
Letter	49	102	38	84	13	42

Source: Bob Franklin, David Murphy, *What New? The Market, Politics
and the Local Press,* 1991.

retested. Secondly, there are its claims to representativeness. By covering
a large number of cases, a broad pattern of representations may be
identified. These patterns provide the data from which explanatory
frameworks may be developed, particularly with respect to the intentions
of the producers and the likely responses of the audience.

For example, the data in Fig. 3.3 can be used to support a pluralistic view of political balance in local newspapers at election time, especially when judged against the political views of the electorate in the constituencies sampled. Other studies using content analysis have been used as evidence of political bias (see the Glasgow Media Group, below) and gender and racial stereotyping.

Criticisms of content analysis

1 Its objectivity may be questioned on the grounds that the categories initially chosen may reflect the researcher's pre-existing values and assumptions about the media. This parallels the kind of bias produced in surveys where the choice and wording of the questions narrows the agenda and shapes the overall response of those questioned.

2 In focusing on the overt or manifest meanings of media content, there is a danger that the covert or latent meanings may be overlooked. This is especially a problem where meanings arise from the particular context of the representation. Thus, for example, counting the number of violent incidents in an episode of television drama may lead to misleading conclusions about the real extent of violence portrayed if it is portrayed in a ritualistic or parodic manner − as in the 1960s television series *Batman* and *The Avengers*. This suggests the need for an approach which is more sensitive to the particular ways in which the media communicate meaning. This approach is semiology.

2 Semiology

As described above, semiology's starting point is the individual media text which comprises a coded set of signs which may be systematically analysed to identify the specific structures of meaning. By subjecting all the textual signs to such close scrutiny, semiology allows us to recognise the ways in which media texts are a social/cultural construction and not natural or timeless. Their mythical and ideological nature can be revealed.

To subject a media text to semiological decoding the methodology involves separating those technical codes particular to a media form, like radio, magazines, etc., from the wider cultural codes such as the setting, characters and props. Each set of signs contains its own signifiers which, collectively, form the overall textual meaning. For a worked example see Fig. 3.4.

Figure 3.4

Figure 3.4
The main cultural signifiers in the advertisement include:
1 The setting: The business district of an American city in the early hours of the morning (the long shadows, deserted streets).
2 The subjects: A young white male and black female are walking arm in arm and engaged in conversation. They are both dressed stylishly and look happy. Trailing behind them is a young male who looks on, and whose appearance is dishevelled.
3 The prop: Prominently displayed and superimposed in the foreground is an enlarged bottle of Jazz eau de toilette aftershave whose contents are coloured gold.

The main technical signifiers include:
1 The photographic codes: The picture is high contrast black and white (apart from the bottle contents); the subjects are framed in a long shot between the buildings, and appear in sharp focus compared to the foreground and background; the strongest lighting and sharpest focus are reserved for the bottle which is also shot from a low angle.
2 The design codes: The composition is dominated by strong vertical and horizontal lines (the buildings, bottle and line below the bottle); the lettering is *sans serif* upper case and black and white apart from the label which is a customised design.

What is signified?
The signs collectively interact to form codes of meaning concerning what qualities of the product are being signified in the advertisement. The most prominent coding is the implied narrative of an encounter or liaison between the couple who have met during the night. The successful male has used Jazz unlike the man going home alone.

They appear to be affluent young professionals with a modern cosmopolitan lifestyle. The theme of Jazz is also reinforced through the black and white couple, lettering, and bottle top, as well as the American urban setting – the home of jazz music. The black and white photographic image signifies a sense of classic style.

The anchorage is written in French to signify continental sophistication and loosely translates 'its good to be jazz' – a message reinforced by the foregrounding of the bottle whose contents contain the promise of such a modern and successful lifestyle.

Criticisms of semiology

1 By focusing on individual media texts, there is a danger that these might be unrepresentative of the typical or dominant patterns within that media form or category.
2 A strength of semiology is to acknowledge the fact that texts may be polysemic, i.e. contain signifiers which are open to several interpretations. Necessarily, this renders any conclusions about a media text's meanings conditional on the audience decoding. A compromise here is to refer to the meanings the text is thought to privilege as the *preferred reading*.

In practice, it is not the case that content analysis and semiological decoding need be seen as alternative or opposite methods. Much depends on the aim of the research but the two approaches can be used in a complementary fashion to study both the general and the particular of media representations.

Constructing social reality

Up until the 1960s, analysis of political representations in the media was dominated by American social scientists who tended to apply a functionalist perspective. This assumed that the media reflected those central values and norms shared by the wider society. This assumption was eventually challenged by sociologists working within the *interactionist* perspective in the study of deviance.

The rules of society were not seen as consensual so much as open to interpretation. What was 'normal' to one group, or subculture, may be 'deviant' for another.

Howard Becker (1963) was influential in popularising the *labelling theory* in which he stated: 'Social groups create deviance by making the rules whose infraction constitutes deviance, and by applying those rules to particular persons and labelling them as outsiders.'

This raised the question of which social groups made the rules and how the labelling occurred? Becker failed to develop a general theory of the origins of labelling other than to suggest 'moral entrepreneurs' who tended to be white, male and middle class. However, he did recognise the media's part in the labelling of deviants when examining how the *Reader's Digest* helped to create a social reaction against marijuana smokers following the outlawing of the drug in the USA in 1937.

Following Becker's example, Stan Cohen (1972) applied the interactionist perspective to the case of the mods and rockers in the mid 1960s, paying particular attention to the media. Cohen argued that the media were instrumental in labelling youth cultural styles in a stereotyped and negative way, thus creating 'folk devils'. The activities of these folk devils, in this case the conflicts between mods and rockers in British seaside resorts, were then portrayed in such a way as to create a *moral panic*. Cohen describes this as when, 'a condition, episode, person or group of persons emerges to become defined as a threat to societal values and interests'. In the last 30 years there have been a series of moral panics with respect to youth cultures.

Cohen saw the media's role as crucial in structuring public awareness of the issue in terms of the causes, extent and control necessary to contain the 'social problem'. In so doing, they helped to *amplify* the problem by creating a social reaction which heightens police activity, court sentencing and public awareness in a vicious escalating circle or *spiral*, which had little relation to the real situation, i.e. in this case the numbers of mods and rockers involved and the rationale for their behaviour.

Cohen strongly emphasised the media's role in creating public concern through a combination of exaggerated distortion, labelling and prediction. To anticipate trouble in itself may help to create a self-fulfilling prophecy as the lure of the media spotlight attracts both the police and potential deviants. In an examination of a more recent moral panic surrounding the 'acid house' dance culture, Sarah Thornton (1995) argues that the condemnation of the media was an essential element in giving the embryonic culture a rebellious authenticity and helping to transform it into a fully fledged youth sub culture. Without such negative media coverage, Thornton claims the acid house culture would have failed to ignite (see Fig. 3.5).

It is clear that any analysis of media reporting of social phenomena needs to start from the premise that, rather than being a 'mirror on reality', the media help to *construct* that social reality.

It is therefore logical to ask whose definition of reality is being represented? One approach adopted by the interactionist perspective has been to examine the attitudes and practices of media professionals, particularly those constructing a daily picture of what is happening 'out there' – the news journalists.

Figure 3.5
Although negative reporting is disparaged, it is subject to anticipation, even aspiration. Positive tabloid coverage, on the other hand, is the subcultural kiss of death. In 1988, *The Sun* briefly celebrated acid house, advising their readers to wear T-shirts emblazoned with smiley faces, the music's coat of arms, in order to 'dazzle your mates with the latest trendy club wear', before they began running hostile exposés. Had the tabloid continued with this happy endorsement of acid house, it is likely the scene would have been aborted and a movement would not have ensued. Similarly, rave culture would probably have lost its force with this second wave of positive reports had it not been followed by further disapproving coverage (about ravers converging on free festivals with 'travellers', namely, nomadic 'hippies' and 'crusties' who travel the countryside in convoys of 'vehicles').

Cultural studies and sociologies of 'moral panic' tend to position youth cultures as innocent victims of negative stigmatization. But mass media 'misunderstanding' is often an objective of certain subcultural industries, rather than an accident of youth's cultural pursuits. 'Moral panic' can therefore be seen as a form of hype orchestrated by culture industries that target the youth market. The music press seemed to understand the acid house phenomenon in this way, arguing that forbidden fruit is more desirable and that prohibition never works. The hysterical reports of the popular press, they argued, amounted to a 'priceless PR campaign' (Q January 1989).

Source: Sarah Thornton, *club Cultures Music, Media and Subcultural Capital,* 1995.

News values

It is a commonly held misconception that events 'happen', and are then mediated to the public via the printed word and the screen, the mediation being mainly technical, i.e. writing or filming the story. Rarely is newsgathering so simple and direct. A comparison of the front pages of Britain's national newspapers on any day of week would reveal that journalists *manufacture* news, not in the sense of fabricating it (although some stories may have little basis in reality), but in the sense of making choices about *what* to cover and *how* to cover news. 'News is people. It is people talking and people doing. Committees and Cabinets and courts are people; so are fires, accidents and planning decisions. They are only news because they involve and affect people.' (Harold Evans, 1963)

This comment from Harold Evans, former editor of *The Times*, reveals one of the most important news values held by journalists: personalisation, i.e. events are seen as the actions of individuals rather than forces. News values refer to what journalists consider as *newsworthy* (see Fig. 3.6 for a full list of key news values).

Figure 3.6
News values
1 *Frequency*
The time-span taken by an event. Murders take very little time and their meaning is quickly arrived at. Hence their frequency fits that of daily newspapers and programmes. On the other hand, economic, social or cultural trends take very much longer to unfold and to be made meaningful: they are outside the frequency of daily papers. Thus they have to be 'marked' (if they are reported at all) by means of devices like the release of reports or statistics on a particular day.
2 *Threshold*
The size of an event. There is a threshold below which an event will not be reported at all (varying in intensity between, for instance, local and national news). And once reported, there is a further threshold of drama: the bigger the story, the more added drama is needed to keep it going. War reporting is an example of this. Already very big news, its coverage is unlikely to increase unless an especially cataclysmic event happens.
3 *Unambiguity*
The clarity of an event. Events don't have to be simple, necessarily (though that helps), but the range of possible meanings must be limited . . .
4 *Meaningfulness*
(a) Cultural proximity: events that accord with the cultural background of the news-gatherers will be seen as more meaningful than others, and so more liable to be selected . . .

(b) Relevance: events in far-off cultures, classes or regions will nevertheless be newsworthy if they impinge on the news-gatherer's 'home' culture – usually in the form of a threat; as with OPEC and the (mostly Arab) countries with oil – their lifestyles, customs and beliefs are suddenly fascinating for Western journalists.

5 *Consonance*

The predictability of, or desire for, an event. If the media expect something to happen, then it will . . .

6 *Unexpectedness*

The unpredictability, or rarity, of an event. Of course it is within the *meaningful* (4) and the *consonant* (5) that the unexpected is to be found. Hence the 'newness' of unexpected events usually gets discovered in thoroughly familiar, expected contexts.

7 *Continuity*

The 'running story'. If an event is covered, it will continue to be covered for some time.

8 *Composition*

The mixture of different kinds of event. If a newspaper or TV bulletin is packed with major foreign stories, a relatively insignificant domestic story will be included to balance the mixture. Alternatively, if a major story is running, other similar events may be selected for inclusion in a 'round-up' of stories on that subject . . .

9 *Reference to élite nations*

Stories about wars, elections and disasters are good examples of this tendency. Wars involving the USA, USSR, or forces explicitly allied to one or the other, will be reported, whereas others go virtually unnoticed . . .

Elections in France, Germany and Italy will receive more coverage that those in Latin America, Africa, etc. And, of course, there is the famous head-count equation for disasters: disasters in Bangladesh, for example, need thousands or hundreds killed to reach the newsworthiness threshold, whereas those in 'élite' countries will be newsworthy with progressive lower body-counts.

10 *Reference to élite persons*

Firstly because it is assumed their actions are more

consequential than the daily activities of ordinarily people — they 'affect our lives'. Secondly, the social activities of élite people can serve as representatives actions — their weddings, opinions, nights out and domestic habits are taken to be of interest to us all, since we too engage in these things . . .

11 *Personalisation*

Events are seen as the actions of people as individuals. Individual people are easier to identify — and to identify with — than structures, forces or institutions: hence 'the government' is often personalised as 'Mrs Thatcher' etc.

12 *Negativity*

Bad news is good news. It is generally *unexpected* (6), *unambiguous* (3), it *happens quickly* (1), it is *consonant* (5) with general expectations about the state of the world, and hence its *threshold* (2) is lower than that for positive news.

Source: John Hartley, *Understanding News*, 1982.

The process of choosing or rejecting stories on the basis of these news values has been referred to as 'gatekeeping', and the journalist most in control of this process is the editor. Editors fulfil what is essentially a filtering role — selecting or 'opening the gate' for some stories, while 'closing the gate' for others as there is usually an excess of material available to fill limited newspaper or broadcasting space (see Fig. 3.7a). Therefore, news values may vary according to the editorial policy of a specific newspaper, e.g. *The Sun* may emphasise personalisation and frequency more than *The Times*. Furthermore, technical considerations may also shape news coverage, so that television often includes a story if video is available or if it is very recent, hence underlining the advantages that it holds over newspapers who print 'yesterday's' news. Television news editors are especially keen to bring us the news 'as it happens' which means live visual coverage, if possible, or, even more dramatic, a news flash which interrupts the evening's viewing. This helps to strengthen the public idea that 'raw news' is brought direct and unmediated to the audience, an idea which the interactionist perspective has exposed to be mythical. News is the result of a social process guided by the news values held by journalists.

Figure 3.7a   The flow of news – inside the office

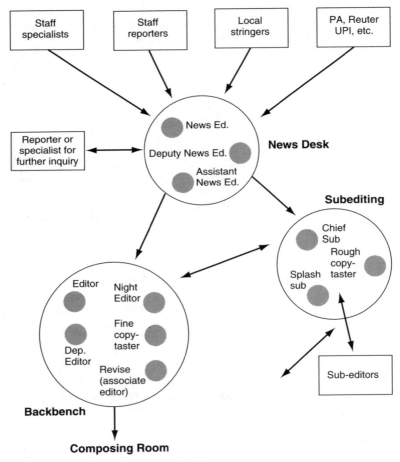

Source: Alistair Hetherington *Newspapers and Television*, 1985.

The origins of news values

Journalists do not work in a social vacuum. While it is important to understand how media professionals define the world, it is also necessary to consider the relationship they have with the rest of society. They are

Figure 3.7b   Determinants of news production

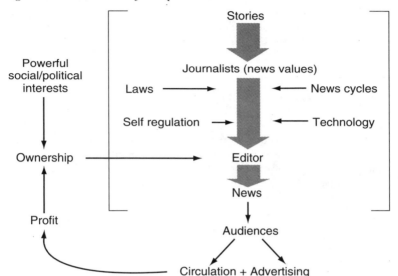

not so independent as to be unaffected by certain social and economic forces.

However, there is no consensus as to which of these forces is the most significant in determining the production of news. (See Fig. 3.7b.)

1. Economic

As outlined in Chapter 2, maximising the audience is a vital goal for most media organisations. A 'good' story is one that is seen as holding the reader's/viewer's attention. Hence the stress on negativity, personalities, drama, at the expenses of background detail, complex causes, etc.

Within TV, American companies found that news programmes became more profitable as they tended towards a 'show', using the format of newsreading teams who had individual 'personalities'. British TV news followed in the same direction with ITV initiating dual news presenters, the BBC having the first female newsreader (Angela Rippon), and newsreaders often being indistingusihable from entertainers.

This emphasis on profitability and pleasing the audience fits the pluralist model of media production. If Britain's tabloid newspapers tend towards a conservative set of news values, this is seen as a reflection of its readers' own prejudices.

2 Institutional

While newspapers are increasingly subject to market pressures, there is still some latitude for journalists to exert an autonomous influence. This is particularly the case with the broadsheet newspapers where more space is available for in-depth feature writing. A newspaper's traditional reputation and identity may also constrain the opportunity to change the editorial formula. Relaunches and significant changes in editorial policy tend to arise only when a newspaper's very existence is in doubt. For example, *Today* newspaper underwent several changes in identity in line with both changes in ownership and a continuing problem of low circulation. In contrast, newspapers like *The Daily Telegraph* and *The Guardian* have been notable for the stability and continuity of their journalistic approach.

In the case of broadcasting, news reporting has been subject to a strong regulatory constraint – the requirement to be politically impartial. This can be seen in the following extract from the BBC Guidelines for Factual Programmes:

BBC GUIDELINES FOR FACTUAL PROGRAMMES
Impartiality
Impartiality lies at the heart of BBC programme making.

- The BBC must serve the nation as a whole.
- This means recognising the differing tastes, views and perspectives in millions of households.
- They have to be served through a very diverse range of programmes.

The makers of objective factual programmes need to be most scrupulous.
- News judgements should be informed by the best expertise.
- Treatment of a story must involve depth of inquiry.
- Beware of easy and prevalent assumptions.

> Viewers and listeners should not be able to gauge from impartial BBC programmes the personal views of presenters and reporters. When a subject is highly contentious only manifestly impartial treatment will describe and analyse events reliably.
>
> - All aspects of the programme – script, questions to interviewees and selection of material – must persuade the audience that the issues have been explored fairly without bias or preconceived conclusion.

Although other terrestrial broadcasters, including ITV and Channel 4, share the same commitment to impartiality, the BBC has a strong sense of being the nation's most authoritative source of news, particularly when it comes to stories of national significance, such as political crises or major disasters.

To judge from audience surveys, this trust in television, and especially in the BBC, is shared by a majority of the population. However, some academic critics of the media argue that *all* news reporting is subject to ideological influence.

3 Ideological

A key underlying assumption in this approach is that the selection and reporting of news is shaped by a certain framework of values and norms held by journalists, but which are largely derived from outside of media organisations.

> If newsmen did not have available – in however routine a way – such cultural 'maps' of the social world, they could not 'make sense' for their audiences of the unusual, unexpected and unpredicted events which form the basic content of what is 'newsworthy'.
>
> Stuart Hall (1978)

These cultural 'maps' or assumptions include ideas that society is largely composed of individuals, is fundamentally meritocratic, and is based on consensus. A functionalist or pluralist perspective would broadly agree with this representation of society, whereas a more critical perspective, as typified by Stuart Hall, would claim that journalists tend to reproduce, if unconsciously, the *ideologies* of those who are most powerful in society.

(a) Centre for Contemporary Cultural Studies (CCCS)

The CCCS in Birmingham University, formerly headed by Stuart Hall, has produced a wealth of material on the media since the early 1970s. The main thesis has concerned the *ideological effect* of the media, which is to shape and organise consensus in what is essentially a class-divided society. The media's (especially TV's) perceived status as neutral, impartial and balanced actually works to create this effect, as it serves to endorse the political system as it stands, i.e. a two-party parliamentary system. Within news and current affairs, balance ensures that there is always a two-sided dialogue and, by inference, that the truth lies somewhere in between.

This also means that issues are debated within certain boundaries (BBC's *Questions Time* might be considered typical of how the debate is framed within the selection of the invited guests who make up the panel). Groups falling outside the parliamentary system are labelled illegitimate, extremist, undemocratic, etc., e.g. the IRA or ecological activists.

The media's role, then, is to help to set the agenda to decide which issues will be examined within what is taken to be a framework of consensus, i.e. the 'national interest'.

In their work, *Policing the Crisis* (1978), Hall and his colleagues applied Gramsci's concept of hegemony to post-war Britain. They argued that, following the period of stability and affluence of the 1950s and early 1960s, Britain entered a period of economic and social crisis when public consent seemed to be weakening (especially in industrial relations), thus threatening ruling class hegemony. In order to win support for stronger powers to control this crisis, it was represented as a crisis of law and order. Hall contended that various separate social issues were transformed into 'moral panics' (e.g. student protests, picketing, mugging) and interconnected so as to appear to be one common problem, the breakdown of law and order, paving the way for changes leading to stronger state control. The media's contribution to this sequence is the access it provided for the *primary definers* of the crisis, those considered legitimate spokespeople, i.e. the government and agencies of social control, the police, courts, etc. These are the people with power, to whom the media naturally turn to make sense of the world, given their own commitment to remain detached and impartial. (See Fig. 3.8 on mugging and the media.)

Figure 3.8
Mugging
So the media do not act their own. Of course, crime is always news, and some papers keep a constant watch on this tantalising topic of crime. But the media also depend on the definers of crime – the police, the courts, the Home Secretary – to identify the main movements in the incidence of crime, so that when you get headlines in the press about crime waves, those headlines depend on the institutional links between those who define and control crime and those who report it as news . . .

The police draw attention to the rise in 'muggings' and the judges comment on that rise when they are delivering sentences, and the media report both. They form a sort of circle with other institutions that are involved, and the 'mugging' topic then gets transferred from the courts and police to the media. At the same time, the way that these other institutional spokesmen, the police and the courts, see the crime becomes the primary definition of 'mugging' in the press . . .

Each aspect of the public debate about 'mugging' passes through the media. They form the link between the definers and controllers, the public and the news.

Now, of course, the media don't express personal opinions about events . . . Television is required by the charters to be objective and impartial. Even in the press, where editorial opinions do get expressed, a distinction is drawn between opinion and fact. But this requirement to be 'objective' means that the media must rely heavily on the official definers. The television reporter, for example, substantiates everything he says by referring to what definers have said, by quoting an authority, and some definers always get quoted: they have a right to be heard. Powerful opinions stand highest in the pyramid of access to the media, and this means that the media naturally incline towards, and tend to reproduce, the definitions of those people who are powerful in the society. The media pick up their definitions first. It is they who define the topic.

You may think that doesn't matter, but there are always alternative points of view, alternative explanations for events. There are few actions, however awful, which are meaningless or absolutely without motive or cause for those people who do them. Accounts which do not fit neatly with the primary definitions do, of course, sometimes also get access to the media. But they do not have access as of right – these opinions come later.

Source: Stuart Hall, *The Listener*, 1 May 1975.

(b) The Glasgow Media Group (GUMG)

A group of academics in Glasgow University, led by John Eldridge and Greg Philo, have been subjecting broadcasters' news coverage to their intense scrutiny for the past 20 years. Their general premise is that television news is inherently biased towards the political 'right' (see Fig. 3.9a). Their argument that journalists use *inferential framework* (unspoken assumptions about what is normal or legitimate) in reporting news is illustrated in their analysis of industrial relations coverage, where stories fit a dominant consensual view that uninterrupted production is a 'good thing' and that strikes are disruptive and harmful. This is reinforced in the language journalists use to describe industrial disputes (see Fig. 3.9b). The language is skewed towards management who exercise control as of right, whereas workers' actions are often made to seem irrational or simply militant.

Figure 3.9a

The journalists' world view

In the period of our study, the news was organised and produced substantially around the views of the dominant political group in our society. We have shown how the views of those who disagree fundamentally with this position, or who offered alternative approaches, were downgraded and underrepresented in the news coverage. This is in stark comparison with the careful explanation and heavy emphasis given to the dominant analysis and the political policies which flowed from it . . .

Our argument, then, is that the world view of journalists will prestructure what is taken to be important or significant. It will do this in two ways. First it will affect the character and content of specific inferential frames used in the news . . . Second, it will set general boundaries on where news is looked for, and on who are the significant individuals the 'important' people to be interviewed, etc.

Source: Glasgow Media Group, 1980.

Figure 3.9b The conceptual organisation of industrial news

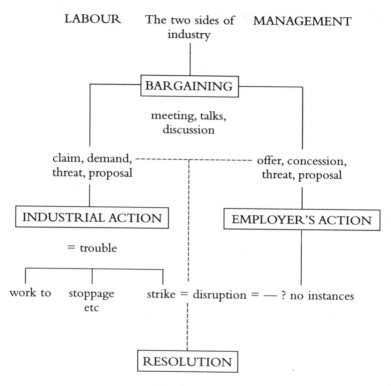

Source: Glasgow University Media Group, *More Bad News*, 1980.

Among their various case studies is the 1984/5 miners' strike in which the GUMG detected a distinctive bias in reporting in favour of the Coal Board and government (GUMG 1986). Their principal evidence for this conclusion is the way in which television news placed a strong emphasis on the drift back to work of striking miners as the dispute progressed. The GUMG argue that this was because of the journalists' willingness to adopt the news agenda and statistics promoted by the Coal Board. A further criticism of the coverage was the exaggerated attention given to violence committed by picketing miners, in contrast to the lack of criticism of police violence and the relative peacefulness of most of the miner's action.

Their analysis of the miner's strike and of television news coverage in general has been challenged by other academics. Anderson and Sharrock (1979) argue that it is the GUMG who are ideologically biased and frustrated because journalists do not employ their left-wing news agenda. On an empirical level, the GUMG research methods and findings have been criticised. Alastair Hetherington (1985) concluded that the television news reporting of the miner's strike was balanced and any misreporting or inaccuracy arose purely because of the normal constraints that journalists experienced – that of working under tight deadlines.

Meanwhile, even the GUMG acknowledge that, aside from television news, current affairs programmes and documentaries do provide space for more complex explanations and alternative political agendas to be considered, even if they might not reach such a large television audience.

The CCCS and GUMG research: a summary

1   Both the CCCS and GUMG have concentrated on the way in which media representations are ideological – they tend towards producing a view of the world which helps to disguise the nature of class-based inequality in society. Being mainly Marxist in their approach, it is not surprising that they regard this ideology as serving to maintain the interests of those with economic power in perpetuating a capitalist economic system (hence GUMG's focus on industrial conflict and the media).

2   In following the tradition of neo-Marxists like Gramsci and Althusser, they have recognised the relative autonomy of the media, i.e. they do not act as propaganda agents or mouthpieces for the capitalist class, but media professionals do have some freedom in which to produce newspapers, TV programmes, etc. In this way, it cannot be assumed that the media will automatically defend such class interests. A careful analysis of content is necessary in search of its ideological meaning. Therefore, it may be possible for messages opposed to ruling class interests to be produced. Periodically the BBC and ITV are attacked by those in power for allowing 'illegitimate', and possibly subversive,

views to be presented. It is clear that, in these situations, journalistic autonomy is overtly constrained by the state. Both the BBC and ITV have been openly criticised by the government for their willingness to represent the IRA perspective during the Northern Ireland conflict. For example, a 1985 BBC documentary, *Real Lives*, which featured a profile of a Sinn Fein/IRA leader, was temporarily banned and re-edited before being broadcast, and many other programmes have been withdrawn or censored by broadcasting controllers for fear of government action. Direct censorship was introduced in 1988 with a broadcast ban on using the voices of members of various 'terrorist' organisations, especially the IRA. This was not lifted until 1995 when there was an IRA ceasefire.

During both the Falklands and Gulf Wars, the Ministry of Defence took control of news coverage by vetting all reports filed by journalists from the war zones. Such explicit external censorship was effectively reinforced by broadcasters generally adopting a policy of self-censorship which ensured that little critical or damaging publicity was produced by the news media. How far this was necessary because of 'national interests' and the morale of the forces, rather than the need for national consensus and public support for the government is a matter of debate. It is clear then that news production is subject to a wide range of influences – economic, ideological and institutional. These influences are illustrated in Figure 3.7b.

Patriarchal ideology

Feminism has made a large impact on media studies in the last decade. Although, as with Marxism, there are differences within feminist theory, feminists share a view that societies are characterised by male domination (patriarchy) over women. This domination enables men to gain at women's expense, particularly in the home where women are tied to a domestic role which exploits them (e.g. housework as a duty) and restricts their opportunities to succeed in the world of paid work.

The question that feminists have tried to answer is why women do not rebel against this oppression. Like Marxists trying to explain the failure of the working class to rebel, they have turned to the concept of ideology. Patriarchal ideology works to represent gender roles, with the division between man as economic provider and woman as emotional provider in the home, as 'natural' and inevitable rather than a product of male power.

Various studies have identified a patriarchal ideology running through the media, whether in children's comics, advertisements or the cinema. One common theme is the persistent way in which women are represented as objects of male desire. In an influential analysis of women's role in Hollywood cinema, Laura Mulvey (1975) argued that females were invariably positioned as passive objects of male gaze, providing pleasure in a way that reproduces the structure of unequal gender relationships in society.

A number of content analyses have confirmed that women are underrepresented in most forms of media (see Fig. 3.10). A further criticism is that when they do appear it is often in a marginalised or inferior manner, such as the hostess on a television game show. This led Gaye Tuchman (1981) to complain that the media engage in 'the

Figure 3.10

FREQUENCY OF WOMEN AND MEN BY TYPE OF
PROGRAMME

	Men	Women	Men %	Women %	Approx ratio of men:women
National news	819	184	82	18	4:1
Factual	1011	489	67	33	2:1
Light entertainment	478	203	70	30	7:3
Sport	145	13	92	8	11:1
Religious	5	4	56	44	3:2
Children's programmes	25	22	53	47	1:1
Fiction	597	402	60	40	3:2
Film	409	176	70	30	7:3
Totals	3489	1493	70	30	7:3

Source: Broadcasting Standards Council, *Perspectives of Women in Television*, 1994.

symbolic annihilation of women' – i.e. that they are absent, marginalised or trivialised. Even when media production is geared to a female audience, feminist critics have argued that traditional ideologies of femininity are reinforced, as for example in Angela McRobbie's account of the best selling adolescent girls' magazine of the 1970s and early 1980s, *Jackie* (see Fig. 3.11).

However, this implies an overly deterministic view of the power of the media over a passive female audience. In the case of *Jackie*, subsequent research by Elizabeth Frazer (1987) into how its readers viewed the magazine revealed a fairly critical and detached response. The girls were conscious of its generic codes and conventions (as a teenage girls' magazine) which led to a lack of realism. Indeed, this may account for the steady decline of its popularity in the 1980s, in contrast to the rapid rise of *Just Seventeen* which embraced a more hard hitting and realistic editorial approach in its treatment of its readers' aspirations and problems, especially in its letters pages. Even in advertising, which has been subject to the strongest criticism concerning gender representations, there has been a distinctive shift in some campaigns away from the more traditional stereotypes (see Fig. 3.12), culminating in Persil's advertising agency declaring in 1996 that the housewife had been permanently banished from its television commercials.

Figure 3.11
The ideology of Jackie
What, then, are the central features of *Jackie* in so far as it presents its readers with an ideology of adolescent femininity? First it sets up, defines and focuses exclusively on 'the personal', locating it as the sphere of *prime* importance to the teenage girl. It presents this as a totality – and by implication all else is of secondary interest to the 'modern girl'. Romance problems, fashion, beauty and pop mark out the limits of the girl's concern – other possibilities are ignored or dismissed.

Second, *Jackie* presents 'romantic individualism' as the ethos, *par excellence*, for the teenage girl. The *Jackie* girl is alone in her quest for love; she refers back to her female peers for advice, comfort and reassurance *only* when she has problems in fulfilling this aim. Female solidarity, or more simply the idea of girls together – in *Jackie* terms – is an unambiguous sign of failure. To achieve self-respect, the girl has to escape the 'bitchy', 'catty', atmosphere of female company and find a boyfriend as fast as possible. But in doing this she has not only to be individualistic in outlook – she has to be prepared to fight ruthlessly – by plotting, intrigue and cunning, to 'trap her man'. Not surprisingly, this independent-mindedness is short-lived. As soon as she finds a 'steady', she must renounce it altogether and capitulate to *his* demands, acknowledging his domination and resigning herself to her own subordination.

Source: A. McRobbie, '*Jackie*, an ideology of adolescent femininity', in B. Waites et al., 1982.

Figure 3.12
What is new, however, is the advertiser's recognition that the perception of the viewer, and especially of the female viewer, has undergone a radical transition in this time. No longer easily coaxed to believe that her life mission is to scrub grates or even to spend dreamy afternoons driving along country lanes, women, it is assumed, will now respond more favourably to constructions that

collude, however superficially, with their upbeat, outgoing perception of their lives. Hence the wink and the joke, the refusal to take motherhood too seriously, that sets the gap between the 1950s Persil advertisements (risible to a contemporary audience in the zealous and class-bound moralizing) and the 1990s Oxo family.

Advertisers, too, always in tune with aspirational thinking, know that women increasingly want to be 'on top'. It is hard to imagine a contemporary advertiser choosing to replay in any straight form the Knight's Castile romantic narrative, with the woman in a purely passive role, awaiting male attention. Romance still features, but it has either been rendered exotic, or spiced with danger. Occasionally, as we have seen, women can step into the shoes of the heroine and get the better of men; a safe strategy in selling products aimed uniquely at women, but deploying it in car advertising is more daring, and, as a means of changing the image of a traditionally masculine drink, bolder still. A recent advertisement for Tennent's Lager depicts four young women on a lunchtime outing sending up the amorous attentions of an Italian waiter. Although the stereotyping of the male allows the sensibilities of traditional Tennent's drinkers to be protected from the ridicule of the young women's laughter, this marks a new approach in lager advertising. Allowing women sporadic triumphs may have begun to blur the gender boundaries, but reversing femininity's value as a malleable sign is not readily accomplished.

Unsettling masculinity's stability as a sign might speed up the pace of change. To date, masculinity has been extended by men appearing foolish (usually in role reversal contexts), occasionally caring (especially of babies), or displaying virile bodies emphasizing their strength and carefully developed physique. If the last reverses the pattern of the 'male gaze', it does not reverse the status of masculinity. Mr Happywoman, delighting in his partner's pleasure, is still some way off.

Source: Myra McDonald, *Representing Woman*, 1995.

One notable area of change in recent years has been the open acknowledgement and representation of female desire. Perhaps the most striking example of this is in the pop world where Madonna, through her pop videos and stage performances, has constructed an image of herself as a sexually empowered and independent woman. Critics have accused her of exploiting sexuality as a commercial strategy. Given her deliberately ambiguous and constantly evolving identity and the playful, postmodern sensibility she applies to most of her work, it is not surprising that feminists and non-feminists alike are divided about how progressive Madonna is as an image of 1990s woman.

The move towards accentuating female sexuality has also been apparent in women's magazines, especially titles competing for young single and economically independent women, e.g. *Cosmopolitan, Company* and *More*. While this focusing on the sexual pro-active female is a significant shift away from the sexual passivity of women traditionally portrayed in the media, it is not necessarily an unqualified endorsement of female independence and power. Myra McDonald (1995) points out that these magazines still remind women that a central aim is to satisfy men. Female assertiveness has its limits. If there is a sexual problem, then the magazines prefer to advise women on the interpersonal and sexual skills which need to be employed rather than confront the issue of the shortcomings of male sexuality.

It would be a mistake to assume that the mainstream media have never provided space for representations of strong and independent

Figure 3.13

women – the British social realist soap opera, from *Coronation Street* in the 1960s and 1970s, through to *EastEnders* and *Brookside* in the 1980s and 1990s, have consistently featured heroic female characters surviving against all the odds, in contrast to the relatively weak and unsympathetic male characters. Soap opera is one of the few media genres in which there is such a high proportion of female characters. Yet even in predominantly 'masculine' genres, such as science fiction and action adventure films, there has been the emergence of a range of action heroines, as in films like *Alien* and *Thelma and Louise*, but these are still very much isolated cases. Meanwhile, despite evidence of a widening range of masculine representations, including more sensitive, emotional images of fatherhood and male insecurity, there is still a preponderance of traditional forms of masculinity, be it the violent aggression of *Reservoir Dogs* or the laddish sexism of *Loaded*.

Racist ideology

Inequalities between racial and ethnic groups have been well documented in official statistics and various social surveys. Racial discrimination has been proven to be a major causal factor and this has been closely linked to *racism*, an ideology of white racial superiority over blacks. Having its roots in the colonial past of Western Europe, this ideology explains white rule in Africa and Asia in terms of white culture as 'civilised' or 'developed' and black culture as 'primitive' or at worst 'savage'. While these images may seem dated, they can still be found in films made during the era of the British Empire, or in the USA during the period of racial segregation in the deep south.

Despite Britain becoming a multicultural country since the Second World War, there has still been a tendency for the media to adhere to negative racial stereotyping. In her analysis of British television representations of racial and ethnic minorities, Angela Barry (1988) argues that three myths have been everpresent. Firstly, the image of the black person as *trouble maker*. A number of news stories have coalesced around the theme of race and troubles. At various stages these have included the problem of immigration numbers and cultural identity, crime on the streets (especially mugging) and race riots.

A second myth identified by Barry is the black person as *entertainer*. At its most patronising was BBC's *Black and White Minstrel Show*, broadcast between 1958 to 1976, which featured white male dancers 'blacked up'. Later on, the sitcom *It Ain't Half Hot Mum* included Indians whose appearance and speech were designed to be quaint and amusing.

Finally, the third of the myths is that of black *dependency*. Periodically, there have been acute crises in Third World, especially African, countries concerning famine and disease. The television coverage, although sympathetic, has tended to focus on the emotive images of emaciated children and the need for Western governmental or charity aid as a solution. Such reportage has largely ignored the more complex causes of the crises, particularly arising from the workings of the global economic system. Instead, this has reinforced the idea that these countries lack the competence to be self-sufficient and can only survive with external support. This perception can easily be transferred to those ethnic minorities living in Britain who are often represented as a burden on the (white) indigenous population (see Fig. 3.14).

During the 1980s it has been possible to identify the emergence of more positive representations which have challenged some of the traditional ideologies embedded in the myths described above. On television, this has been facilitated by a commitment to represent ethnic minority cultural interests on Channel 4 and BBC 2. Soap operas (with the notable exception of *Coronation Street*) have also begun to reflect the ethnic diversity of Britain's urban neighbourhoods.

Meanwhile, as media output increasingly fragments in the search for niche audiences, so there has developed a range of specialist productions made by and for ethnic minority audiences. These include radio stations, newspapers and magazines. The most prolific form of black media expression in the last decade has been in popular music, especially rap music. Given that the most disaffected and marginalised members of minority groups tend to be its youth, rap has acted as a focus for voicing this alienation. It has made its greatest impact in America, where in its gangsta rap form it has led to a (white) backlash from those in authority. Douglas Kellner analyses the appeal of rap music to black American youth and argues that many of its critics have interpreted the lyrics and posturing of the performers too literally while overlooking the diversity of messages and stances adopted within rap music (see Fig. 3.15).

Stereotypes – an ideological force?

Concern about the (mis)representation of minority groups (be they women, blacks or youth) in the media has often focused on negative

Figure 3.14

stereotyping, a process whereby damaging labels are applied to whole groups, e.g. that all black urban youths are drug dealers. However, the implication that, by avoiding using stereotypes, media representations of minorities will be transformed into a positive force is too simplistic.

Figure 3.15

One of the first things that one notices when listening to contemporary rap is how it is a form of articulating identity and self-assertion in an environment increasingly hostile to African-Americans. The rap artists frequently call attention to themselves and use their music to affirm their own identity. This may border on narcissism and a materialism that brags of its record sales and material possessions, but it also a mode of self-assertion in an environment hostile to any form of African-American self-expression. The rap artists are saying: Hey, we're here! Listen to us and hear what we are telling you!

The frequently collective nature of rap groups, on one hand, decenters individualism for group identity, but often affirms both the individual and group identity, as individual rappers call attention to themselves as distinct voices, but then re-submerge themselves into groups. Like graffiti artists, who took on nicknames, rap artists often utilize a pseudonym, like Chuck D or Snoop Doggie Dogg, to signify either the anonymity of black voices, or the need to take on another persona to express their concerns. The name serves as a mask in the tradition of African culture and signifies, on some occasions, that the rapper is speaking for the group, or community, as well as themselves.

Rap thus gives expression to very specific voices who have been left out of mainstream culture and the rap artists are concerned to tell you who they are, to let you know where they are coming from and what they have on their mind. Public Enemy's music constantly refrains the group's name in the background of the songs, and the group name itself is an expression of their outsider status and rebellion against mainstream culture. It plays on the sense that black youth are perceived as a "public enemy" in the society at large. Their name also signifies that they are emerging into the public sphere, into mainstream culture, as an enemy, as an outsider, as a disruptive force. They also frequently affirm themselves as "Public Enemy Number One," calling attention to themselves as a threat and danger to the mainstream . . .

Indeed, there is now a coherent tradition of rap with its icons, hierarchies, typologies, legends, and villains. Rap has a private language and slang with its homies or homeboys (pals from the neighbourhood), crews and posses (i.e. the rap team), technical music lingo, expressions like "dope" and "fly" (which are positive), and often ritual obscenity and insider pejoratives. Terms like "gangs" often function metaphorically to describe the crew of the rap group and terms like "bad" signify "cool," or "good," thus reversing its ordinary connotations. Such a complex linguistic form requires learning a language and interpreting the many layers of meaning and signification.

Source: Douglas Kellner, *Media Culture*, 1995.

Firstly, as pointed out by commentators such as Tessa Perkins (1979), stereotypes are not one-dimensional distortions of reality. In order to gain credibility and widespread cultural currency, they usually contain an element of truth. For example, black male youths in American inner cities are more likely to engage in drug dealing and use of guns, as represented in a sympathetic film, *Boyz'n the Hood*. The most powerful stereotypes tend to be rooted in a degree of reality which is then naturalised rather than questioned in order to pass judgement about the inevitability of such a situation or behaviour.

Media texts often contain stereotypes simply because of the need for economy. Thirty-second television commercials or even thirty-minute situation comedies often need shorthand (stereotypical) characters and situations to achieve quick audience recognition. The danger is that researchers look to identify stereotypes within relatively complex media texts, in which little attention is paid to the *function* of the stereotype within the narrative. Is the audience invited to denigrate, laugh at, or possibly identify with, the character? In the postmodern media, stereotypes are increasingly included for the purposes of irony and parody.

It is unrealistic to expect the media to exclude stereotypes in the search for a more authentic and accurate portrayal of the world, even assuming there could be consensus as to what is an authentic or accurate picture of reality. Most media texts are constructed with the aim of creating a heightened form of realism which includes a large degree of fantasy. If there is value in charting the patterns of media stereotypes, it lies in identifying how and why such stereotypes have evolved over time as they will continue to exist as an integral part of media representations.

4 New technologies

As the twentieth century draws to a close, it seems that technological development is ever accelerating. New communication technologies have rapidly emerged as a consequence of digitalisation – the processing of information in digital form within computerised microchips. Such chips have been at the heart of what has been called a 'communications revolution' to which profound social and political implications have been attributed. The assumption that technologies inevitably create significant social changes has been at the heart of what has been called *technological determinism*.

Raymond Williams (1974) defined the theory quite succinctly:

'New technologies are discovered, by an essentially internal process of research and development, which then sets the conditions for social change and progress. Progress, in particular, is the history of these inventions, which 'created the modern world'. The effects of the technologies, whether direct or indirect, foreseen or unforeseen, are as it were the rest of history. The steam engine, the automobile, television, the atomic bomb, have made modern man and the modern condition.'

Typical of this approach to analysing the effects of new communications technologies is Marshall McLuhan. Writing in the 1960s, he speculated that satellite telecommunications would contribute to the growth of the 'global village', a world in which cultural differences would dissolve (for an assessment of this theory, see pages 96–101). Contrary to McLuhan's claim that technology itself is the key variable in determining social responses ('The medium is the message'), the key issue is how the technology is controlled and used within a society.

In tracing the development of new forms of media communication from newspapers to television, Raymond Williams argues that the primary explanation for their emergence is the stimulation provided by new social needs. With respect to press, their greatest development occurred in the last century as a response to the profound social changes associated with urbanisation and industralisation. Such changes created anxiety and controversy and a need for information and explanation which could not be met by existing institutions like the Church. The struggle for democracy gave further impetus to newspaper readership. In the case of photography, Williams claims that the increasing pace of social change and population mobility meant that photographs became popular as a valued point of personal reference – a way of capturing a lost world and separated relationships.

Finally, with broadcasting, the key change which inspired the development of, first, radio and, later, television as a mass medium of communication was what Williams calls mobile privatisation. This refers to the growing separation of home life from other forms of social activity rooted in work and community. Despite the clear inferiority of television as a visual medium compared to cinema, by the 1950s there was a strong desire for entertainment and information to be received in the domestic privacy of the evermore comfortable homes enjoyed by large numbers of the British population. The technologies of radio and television evolved prior to any clearly identified conception of need and content. It was the general social need that significantly shaped the growth of broadcasting as a mass form of communication.

This is not to say that technological developments are simply a result of newly defined social needs. Economic factors, such as the costs and profitability of new technologies, and political factors, such as the need to control or facilitate access to such technologies, are also important. What is apparent is that new technologies do not automatically create their own momentum which is inevitable or predictable. There have been numerous new media technologies which have been heralded as revolutionary but which subsequently have failed to stimulate public interest and are now regarded as obsolescent or redundant.

In the 1970s quadraphonic (four-track) music sound systems were hailed as the successor to stereo sound, and eight-track music cartridges briefly dawned as the new format to supersede audio cassettes. Both innovations rapidly disappeared, despite extensive marketing. More recently, laser discs and digital cassette players have failed to repay their huge investment costs. In contrast, some technological developments have proved far more popular than was anticipated. For example, the huge success of the Walkman took the electronics industry by surprise in the early 1980s. Consequently, there needs to be considerable caution when speculating about the potential impact of new media technologies.

Towards a more democratic society

In the past 15 years, a number of new technological developments have been occurring within the media industries, the consequences of which are still unfolding. When considering the overall impact of these new technologies on media production and consumption, it is clear that no consensus exists as to whether there will be an overall net social gain.

Those who take an optimistic view of new media technologies tend to emphasise the likely social benefits which will accrue to ordinary people. Increased access to information, improved choice of entertainment and the ability to use the technologies in an active, empowering manner are the main claims made by what has been called the *neophiliac* model.

In contrast, the *cultural pessimists* identify very different outcomes arising from new media technologies. Drawing on what is essentially a Marxist political economy model (see pages 22–26), the trend towards vertical integration of media production, coupled with the convergence of digitally based technologies, means that the large multinational media corporations will become even more powerful. Most of the major media corporations are either merging or forming alliances with electronics and telecommunications companies in order to fully exploit the commercial potential of the new media technologies. In addition, the problems of regulating and controlling these new technologies mean that market forces become ever stronger, creating a growing inequality between the 'information rich' and the 'information poor' (see Fig. 4.1).

Statistics produced by the US Census Bureau for America show a similar pattern, with access to computers being heavily biased towards upper income, educated households. For example, in 1995 white households with income above $75,000 are three times more likely to own a computer than households with incomes between $25,000 to $30,000.

In order to assess the validity of these differing claims, recent developments in specific media technologies will be examined.

Video

Although videotape has been available for professional television production since the 1950s, it was not until the 1980s that it became widely affordable in the form of video cassette recorders (VCRs) and video camcorders. Prior to its appearance on the domestic market, it had proved a great asset in television, allowing much greater flexibility of image control and editing, e.g. the action replay in sports coverage. By linking video to computer software, special graphic effects could be

Figure 4.1
CONSUMER DURABLES BY ECONOMIC ACTIVITY STATUS OF HEAD OF HOUSEHOLD (GREAT BRITAIN 1994)

Consumer durables	Socio-economic group of head of household*								Economically inactive heads
	Economically active heads								
	Professional	*Employers and managers*	*Intermediate non-manual*	*Junior non-manual*	*Skilled manual and own account non-professional*	*Semi-skilled manual and personal service*	*Unskilled manual*	*Total*	
Percentage of households with:									
Television									
colour	98	99	97	96	98	96	98	98	95
b/w	1	0	2	2	1	2	2	1	3
Video recorder	89	94	87	87	92	85	82	90	57
CD player	73	70	66	56	59	49	40	61	24
Home computer	34	47	38	25	30	21	16	34	9
Telephone	99	98	95	92	92	85	75	93	88

* Excluding members of the Armed Forces, and economically active full-time students and those who were unemployed and had never worked.

Source: General Household Survey, 1994.

produced and these quickly became apparent in television title sequences, advertising and music videos.

As video cameras have shrunk in size, their portability has become a significant advantage over traditional film cameras. This has been evident in the increased employment of video cameras in news and documentary production. One-person electronic news gathering (ENG) is now a feature of much television news gathering, meaning that mobility and access are greatly enhanced (as well as costing much less than conventional news production teams).

However, it is the application of video to independent and domestic production, via the camcorder, that has created the greatest interest. There have always been individuals and groups wishing to film and distribute their own visual records of events or artistic ventures, but with the advent of video technology, the opportunity to engage in 'film' making has been made available to millions, such is the technical ease and relative cheapness with which videos can be produced. Naturally, the vast majority of videos made are purely for domestic consumption, but it has been shown that independent, or DIY, video can achieve much larger audiences, including mainstream television.

During the 1990s, there have been numerous examples of DIY/independent videos appearing on British television. These range from comedy series such as *You've Been Framed* to *Videodiaries*, a series of personal documentaries.

In the case of *You've Been Framed*, the selection and editorial control of the videos remain in the hands of the television professionals who are simply exploiting the entertainment value of domestic 'accidents'. Parallel to this is the occasional use of domestic video recordings of incidents deemed newsworthy (perhaps the most famous example being the 1991 video recording of the Los Angeles police beating of Rodney King, a black suspect).

Meanwhile, *Videodiaries*, a BBC2 documentary series, demonstrates the possibilities of empowering amateur video makers with access to a mass audience. Editorial control in this case is left almost exclusively in the hands of the subject. Although this level of access to mainstream television is relatively rare, many interest groups have realised the potential of recording their case on video and using it as a campaigning strategy. In some cases, when packaged as a video news release (VNR), some organisations, like Greenpeace, have managed to gain access to television news programmes. More typically, such *social action* video production has been distributed in alternative ways, often providing a contrasting perspective to that made available in the mainstream media.

In 1984–5, during the miners' strike, the miners produced and distributed The Miners Campaign Videotapes, a series of videos designed to tell the 'real story' of the strike, which was not appearing on television or in the press.

Such video news recordings have helped to support a form of 'resistance culture'.

It may be that future developments in cable television could provide additional opportunities for broadcasting independent videos. Already, in the USA, most major cities are required to provide at least one access channel on cable services for such videos, and there is every possibility that cable franchises in Britain may make available similar space for local groups to go on air.

Outside of Britain, grassroots video production has proved its potential as a democratic tool. especially in countries with authoritarian governments who have strong control of the national media. When videos of state tyranny are secretly recorded and smuggled abroad, it can prove a powerful weapon in undermining foreign support and thus help to create pressure for reform. It is evident that the white-controlled apartheid system of South Africa was weakened by the continuous availability of video footage showing the oppresiveness of the system and the black resistance in the townships during the 1980s.

Figure 4.2
BRITAIN'S "residence culture" has developed its own alternative news network. The growing band of anti-road campaigners, animal welfare demonstrators, hunt saboteurs and others taking direct action to protest outside the democratic process is now being filmed by specially-trained sympathisers with video cameras.

Their dramatic footage is used to defend protesters in court, and sold to television news companies hungry for first-hand pictures. It is also distributed through Undercurrents, a video series claiming to show "the news that isn't on the news" and designed to recruit new activists.

Far more people are involved in "grassroots, radical, environmental and social justice activism" than anybody realises, says Thomas Harding, a director of Small World, the non-profit company that makes and mails out Undercurrents.

Source: Independent on Sunday, 5 February 1995.

By the end of the 1980s, the majority of households in Britain owned a video cassette recorder and, although few people acquire independent/DIY videos for domestic consumption, the VCR has certainly been empowering in facilitating timeshifting of television programmes and rental of films. As a result, VCR owners can now create their own television schedules of favourite programmes and films. Groups who are less well served by mainstream television and Hollywood films can access videos aimed at minority cultures, such as Asian ethnic groups, who have the highest rate of video rental per household in Britain.

Nevertheless, it remains a fact that about a quarter of households in Britain do not own a video recorder, and in many cases this is because of low income.

Desktop Publishing

The print media have been experiencing their own digital 'revolution' since the 1980s. Computerised page make-up and plate making, coupled with facsimile transmission to printing plants, seemed to open up the possibility of the newspaper industry becoming accessible to groups without the large resources of the traditional Fleet Street publishers. It is true that several new 'hi tech' national newspaper were launched between 1986 and 1990, including *Today* (1986), *The Independent* (1986), *The News On Sunday* (1987), *The Post* (1988) and *The Correspondent* (1989). Of these, only *The Independent* still survived in 1995, and this was losing money, leading to its takeover by larger publishing companies. The failure of such new titles is testimony to the continued high cost of publishing newspapers, especially the need to invest substantial sums in marketing newspapers in a very competitive and gradually declining industry. The real beneficiaries of new technology have been the existing publishers, such as Rupert Murdoch's News Corporation which has been able to cut costs by making hundreds of skilled print workers redundant and moving production out of Fleet Street to new computerised premises elsewhere.

Where new technology in the print media has made a genuine impact is in magazine publishing where new desktop publishing processes, utilising design software, colour image scanners and laser printers, have enabled DIY magazine production at a fraction of the cost previously required. Every cultural interest or political group can now design and produce publications of a standard equivalent to professional publishers. While much of this output has been on a relatively small scale, such as the fanzine culture (see Fig. 4.3), it has contributed to a proliferation in the range of magazine titles becoming available, some of which have been commercially successful. The main impediments to profitability remain, as ever, attracting advertising revenue and gaining access to the highly integrated chains of high street retail outlets, such as W H Smith and John Menzies.

Cable and satellite television

Despite having very different distribution systems, cable and satellite technologies share many similar issues in terms of their likely impact on media production and consumption. Their main selling point has been the increased number of channels available to subscribers. During the 1990s the number of satellite channels has risen steadily and, with the planned introduction of digital services in 1997, over 100 channels seems a real possibility. Most cable subscribers also have access to satellite channels as well as additional, often local, channels specific to each cable franchise. It would seem reasonable to claim that the viewer has benefited in being able to choose from this plethora of new channels.

It is certainly true that certain interests are lavishly catered for on satellite/cable television. Prominent examples include sport, films, children's cartoons, and pop music. As the number of channels increases, so the trend towards *narrowcasting* has developed, whereby specialist, or niche, audiences are carefully targeted. Cable television is more effective at this, with its ability to target audiences locally, such as ethnic minorities (e.g. *Asia Vision* and *Identity* – for Afro-Caribbeans) and community channels.

However, critics of satellite/cable television have argued that this seeming abundance of choice is not necessarily beneficial to viewers. Despite the huge increase in the number of channels broadcasting, the actual average amount of television viewing has not increased – in fact, there has been a gradual decrease (see Fig. 4.4). Consequently, each new channel is struggling to achieve a viable audience, and existing terrestrial channels are steadily losing their audience share. This is putting a financial squeeze on most companies who are having to cut cost which, in turn, means less investment in programmes. Primetime drama on BBC or ITV can cost over £500,000 per hour to produce. In contrast, some cable or satellite channels can cost as little as £2,000 per hour (e.g. Live TV on cable).

Figure 4.3

RADIOHEAD
WORLD SERVICE
F A N Z I N E

ISSUE 2 £2.50   OCT-DEC '95

This has obvious implications for the production quality and type of programming that can be afforded. A high proportion of the content of the additional channels being offered on cable and satellite television is acquired, often imported, material which has been recycled. Unlike, say, the BBC and Channel 4, little programming which is innovative or reflective of distinctly British cultural interests has been evident.

Figure. 4.4

Hours viewed per person in homes with satellite or cable TV

Channel/ sector	1995 (hours)	Share per cent	Change 95/94 (mins)	1994 (hours)	Share per cent	1993 (hours)	Share per cent
All television	24.88	100.0	−32	25.41	100.0	26.90	100.0
BBC 1	5.91	23.7	−17	6.19	24.4	6.58	24.5
BBC 2	1.61	6.5	3	1.57	6.2	1.76	6.5
BBC total	7.52	30.2	−14	7.76	30.5	8.34	31.0
ITV	7.02	28.2	−38	7.65	30.1	8.21	30.5
Channel 4	1.80	7.2	2	1.76	6.9	1.94	7.2
Independent television	8.82	35.4	−36	9.42	37.1	10.15	37.7
Terrestrial total	16.33	65.6	−50	17.17	67.6	18.49	68.7
Sky One ◊	1.23	4.9	−8	1.37	5.4	1.88	7.0
Sky News ◊	0.37	1.5	4	0.30	1.2	0.34	1.3
Sky Sports	0.95	3.8	4	0.89	3.5	0.90	3.3
Movie Channel	0.79	3.2	−4	0.87	3.4	0.89	3.3
Sky Movies	0.86	3.4	−7	0.97	3.8	1.27	4.7
Sky Movies Gold	0.19	0.8	3	0.15	0.6	0.16	0.6
Other Sky ◊•	0.19	0.8	−	0.05 □	−	○	−
BSkyB total	4.59	18.5	0	4.59	18.1	5.45	20.3
Bravo◊/EBN ■/ Playboy ■	0.17	0.7	0	0.17	0.7	0.09	0.3
Country Music Television ◊	0.05	0.2	1	0.04 □	−	○	−
Discovery ◊/ Learning Channel ◊	0.24	1.0	1	0.21	0.8	0.11	0.4
Disney Channel ◆	0.09 □	−	−	○	−	○	−
Eurosport	0.25	1.0	0	0.25	1.0	○	−
MTV Europe ◊	0.24	1.0	−4	0.31	1.2	0.37	1.4
Nickelodeon/ Paramount ■	0.37	1.5	5	0.28	1.1	0.04 □	−
TCC ◊	0.19	0.7	1	0.18	0.7	0.32	1.2
Family Channel ◊	0.10	0.4	1	0.09	0.3	0.05 □	−

Channel/ sector	1995 (hours)	Share per cent	Change 95/94 (mins)	1994 (hours)	Share per cent	1993 (hours)	Share per cent
TNT/Cartoon Network	0.62	2.5	6	0.51	2.0	0.15 □	–
UK Gold ◊	0.60	2.4	–5	0.68	2.7	0.76 □	2.8
UK Living ◊	0.17	0.7	1	0.14	0.6	0.04 □	–
VH-1 ◊	0.17	0.7	–	0.05 □	–	○	–
Lifetime	○	–	–	○	–	0.02 □	–
Screensport	○	–	–	○	–	0.03 □	–
Others total	3.25	13.1	21	2.94	11.4	1.98	7.4
◊ Satellite Multi Channels	3.52	14.1	–1	3.53	13.9	□	–
Astra total	7.82	31.4	20	7.48	29.4	7.44	27.6
Non-Astra	0.73	2.9	–1	0.76	3.0	0.98	3.6
Non-terrestrial	8.55	34.4	19	8.24	32.4	8.42	1.3
Homes reached (millions, average)	4.4	19.4	17.6	3.7	16.5	3.2	14.6
Viewers reached (millions, average)	12.9	24.2	17.5	10.9	20.6	9.6	18.2
Satellite share of all viewing (%)	8.5				6.8	6.1	

□ On air part year only. ○ Not on air.
• Sky Sports 2, Sky Soap, Sky Travel, History Channel, Sci Fi Channel, Sky Sports Gold.
■ From 1 November. ◆ From 1 October.Source: BARB. Compiled by William Phillips
Source: Broadcast, February 23 1996.

The main anxiety expressed by those critical of the cable/satellite services is over the shift away from public service principles, which have underpinned terrestrial broadcasting, towards commercial market-driven forces. The danger is that a system geared to meeting a broad spectrum of interests and needs at a relatively low cost (the licence fee) is being sacrificed for a system geared to meeting the needs of those most able to pay (the subscription fees and installation of equipment). Sporting events like Premier League football and world boxing title fights have been acquired for exclusive transmission on BSkyB and, as such companies become more profitable, popular drama series may follow suit.

There has been a symbolic attempt to protect the right of public access to the most popular sporting fixtures, such as Wimbledon, the FA Cup Final, etc., by making them 'listed events', preventing them from being transferred to subscription or pay per view cable/satellite channels.

However, regulatory control of such services is modest compared to terrestrial services. BSkyB is virtually a monopoly provider of satellite television in Britain and there is no safeguard against it adopting a partisan political stance (like many newspapers owned by News Corporation, BSkyB's parent company). Most satellite and cable channels are owned by large media corporations with particular vested interests, often based outside of Britain. One concern is that these new services are part of a global trend towards cultural homogeneity which will asphyxiate the distinctive national broadcasting culture which has been shaped by public service principles (this globalising tendency is discussed below).

As of 1996, it is not clear whether satellite and/or cable television will manage to achieve market domination. During the past five years, the number of subscribers to BSkyB has risen from 1 million to approximately 4.5 million (although reliable figures are hard to establish). Added to these are over 1 million cable subscribers who can receive both satellite and cable services, which means that about 25 per cent of the population have access to satellite television. It is estimated that, by the year 2000, this will rise to approximately 50 per cent of the population, with cable likely to have caught up or overtaken satellite in terms of the number of homes connected. However, such forecasts are very speculative, as much depends on whether people's resistance to receiving these new technologies changes significantly in the near future. Currently, only about 20 per cent of homes passed by cable choose to be connected and about half of those surveyed claim that they have no intentions of opting for satellite or cable television in the future. Much may depend on the potential attractions provided by even newer technological developments discussed below.

Digital and interactive television

By compressing analogue television signals into digital form, it is possible to squeeze many more channels into a given frequency space. Both terrestrial and satellite broadcasters expect to be able to offer additional digital channels during 1997. Estimates range from 20–30 more terrestrial channels and up to 200 satellite channels.

Interactive television provides opportunities for viewers to make choices additional to the current options of flicking between channels, adjusting the volume, etc. This is made possible because the television services are delivered by broadband cable to the viewer via a set top decoder and handset which allow him or her to issue instructions and exercise more control over what is viewed. These choices include:

1 selecting schedules, or video on demand. This might involve choosing from a menu of different programmes such as films, cartoons, videogames, etc.
2 selecting programme options. This might include choosing particular camera angles, action replays, requesting supplementary textual information, etc.
3 participatory shows. Viewers can join in games as contestants or take part in studio votes.

Most of these services are at the experimental or pioneering stage and will require huge capital investment before becoming widely available. In order to recoup these costs it is likely that there will be an emphasis on commercial transactional services, such as home shopping, banking, insurance, etc., being a central feature of what is delivered. In America, the first interactive television station, Tele TV, compiles a database of its viewers' television diet which it then makes available to advertisers who can use the data to target would-be consumers personally with interactive 'infomercials' (extended advertisements with interactive options).

It is uncertain whether viewers will be willing, or able, to pay for the decoders or new television sets needed for digital and interactive television. There is little evidence that the new channels will provide a meaningful extension to viewing choice, in so far as they are likely to be dominated by variations on the most popular formats – films, sport, 'gold' repeats, etc. It also remains open to debate as to whether viewers are keen to become more participatory in their mode of viewing.

The Internet

This comprises a 'World Wide Web' of millions of 'pages' of information stored on computers around the world. These 'pages' may contain printed text, images, music, even video clips. Any computer can log on to the Internet via a modem, and multimedia computers enable the full range of content to be accessed and downloaded. It has the technological potential eventually to carry all forms of media production, from newspapers and magazines to television and films.

Supporters of the Internet claim that it offers a radical new means of achieving an open and democratic communication system by enabling ordinary people actively to produce and receive information and entertainment regardless of its origin or destination. State censorship is difficult to enforce because of the proliferation of computers and the problems of tracing who is originating or receiving the information. Thus, authoritarian or repressive governments may find themselves embarrassed by the free flow of politically damaging information. More generally, the Internet can facilitate the formation and development of global interest groups who can use the web collectively to gain strength and build a shared sense of identity (see Fig. 4.5).

Others are more sceptical of these claims and point to potential damage in the flourishing of pornography, already evident in much of the output to date. Another concern is that groups who are essentially anti-democratic, such as neo-Nazis, have already been identified on the Internet. Furthermore, the system is not completely free from commercial exploitation, as access to the Internet in countries like America is ultimately controlled by telecommunications companies and, as business interests begin to participate more vigorously, it seems likely that higher costs will be imposed on those creating the most 'traffic' on the network.

Finally, to return to the argument concerning the information rich and poor (see Fig. 4.1), any advantages which may arise from the new technologies like the Internet have to be weighed against the problems of accessing such technologies for many people, whether they are due to income, education or geography. For example, South Africa is one of the fastest growing Internet markets in the world, yet less than one in 1,000 of its black population owns a phone.

Global media

New media technologies, such as satellite television and the Internet, are helping to accelerate the trend towards the globalisation of the media, a process whereby the same text, be it a Michael Jackson album or a Disney film, is available to audiences in every continent. Media producers often now think in terms of a world market for their films, music, etc., and most of the biggest media corporations have interests in several continents (see Fig. 2.6 on News Corporation). Writing in the 1960s, Marshall McLuhan (1964) anticipated that the simultaneous availability of media communication across the world would create a 'global village', a view echoed by Ed Turner, Head of News at CNN when he claimed that the American satellite news service was 'the towncrier of the global

Figure 4.5

village'. Given that approximately only 2 per cent of the population of Africa own a television set, there is a long way to go before a 'global village' connected by media technologies is a realistic prospect. A more seriously debated proposition concerning the globalisation of the media is that of media imperialism.

Media imperialism

Sociologists and anthropologists have for many years discussed the notion that, following economic imperialism, which was central to the West's colonisation of Africa and Asia in the nineteenth century, there has since been a growth of cultural imperialism, whereby authentic, traditional and local cultures in many parts of the world have been replaced by imported, mainly American and Western European, culture. Central to this process is the role of the media. Consequently, rather than *cultural imperialism*, the concept of media imperialism is often used. A much quoted definition of media imperialism is provided by Oliver Boyd-Barrett (1977).

'The process whereby the ownership, structure, distribution or content of the media in any one country are subject to external pressures from the media interests of any other country or countries without proportionate reciprocation of influence by the country so affected.'

Put more simply, the Western (especially American) media have succeeded in penetrating and colonising those countries (usually with low levels of economic development) because of their superior economic and political power. Boyd-Barrett argues that the less developed countries have been dependent for growth on Western technology and capital and have thus been likely to adopt their models of media organisation and practice, either due to the direct transference of Western media systems or simply through being role models of how it should be done.

One key aspect of the Western model is the use of the advertising of consumer goods as a principal source of revenue. The products and services advertised are very often Western in origin or ownership. This has been seen as a form of ideological endorsement of Western consumerism and capitalism's ability to deliver the 'good life' (a process sometimes referred to as 'coca-colonisation').

In contrast to countries like Britain or America, audiences in these 'Third World' countries are thought to be more vulnerable to such advertising, because of, firstly, minimal regulatory controls, e.g. for cigarette advertising, and, secondly, such audiences are likely to be less 'literate' or sophisticated about reading and resisting the pleasures and rewards promised in the advertisements.

Western media penetration

Next to aircraft, the most profitable export of any American industry in the 1990s has been entertainment (estimated to be worth $5.6 billion in 1993). Perhaps the most renowned element of this is Hollywood, where films have dominated the world cinema market for decades. Even Europe, with its own indigenous film industries, has succumbed to the popular appeal of Hollywood films whose European market share varies between 60–90 per cent (*Screen Digest*, 1993). With production and marketing budgets averaging over $40 million, it is difficult for local film industries to compete effectively with Hollywood.

Such advantages in infrastructure are also found in television where America and Western Europe account for most of the programmes exported abroad. For example, about a third of all television programmes in Asia and the Pacific are imported (Reeves, 1993). Once television productions have made a profit within America, it is possible to sell them abroad at knock down prices which can easily undercut the cost of making home grown programmes, even with much lower production values (see Fig. 4.6).

Figure 4.6

TOP 10 INTERNATIONALLY SOLD TV PROGRAMMES

September 1990 to September 1991

Title	Distributor	Number of Territories
Teenage Mutant Ninja Turtles	Westinghouse	100+
Academy Awards	ABC	100+
Murder, She Wrote	MCA	80+
LA Law	20th Century Fox	75
Moonlighting	ABC	73
Twin Peaks	Worldvision	72
America's Funniest Home Videos	ABC	68
Doogie Howser MD	20th Century Fox	62
The Simpsons	20th Century Fox	60
Beverley Hills 90210	Worldvision	51

* By the number of territories sold to or relicensed in, excluding feature films and made-for-television films.

Source: Television Week, 3–9 October 1991.

More recently, television programmes originating as specialised formats for American cable and satellite channels have been exploited or franchised across the globe. The two best known examples are CNN, a 24-hour news service, and MTV, a music service built around pop videos. MTV, which began in America in 1981, now has seven separate global services, including MTV Europe (reaching 37 countries) and MTV Asia (reading 60 countries).

The success of CNN in becoming the world's most available television news services (watched by both Saddam Hussein and President Bush during the 1991 Gulf War) is typical of the success of Western companies in producing and selling news as a commodity. Of the five agencies which supply international news in bulk, only Russia's Tass is not Western. The remaining four (AP, UPI, Reuters and Agence France-Presse) send out an estimated 34 million words a day and claim to service 90 per cent of the world's newspapers, radio and television states (Smith, 1980). Yet nearly two thirds of their correspondents are based in America or Europe. This lends weight to the claim that such news agencies are significantly biased towards a Western perspective in interpreting news stories.

Media imperialism – a critical assessment

Variations in flow

The assertion that media output flows only from the advanced Western capitalist countries to the rest of the world is overly simplistic. A closer examination of media 'exports' would reveal a considerable amount of regional exchange of media production. Two examples of such regional groupings of countries include Brazil, Mexico and other Latin American countries, and the Middle Eastern Arab countries. There is also considerable variation in the degree to which individual countries import media production. The two largest populated countries, China and India, tend to originate most of their own media production, including film industries whose output exceeds that of Hollywood. The ability of such indigenous media industries to survive and flourish is largely due to the fact that they are rooted in the traditional national and local cultures of such countries, whereas imported Western media often contain unfamiliar and alien cultural values and beliefs.

Cultural adaptation and resistance

In order to be successful in different cultural settings, Western media forms and texts very often need to be adapted to fit familiar codes and conventions of the national or local media. A good example is that of soap opera. Originating on American radio in the 1940s, the genre has spread throughout the globe but, in doing so, has been reworked to reflect specific cultural situations. In Brazil, where they are known as telenovellos, soaps have been particularly popular. These serials typically comprise stories which focus on the social problems arising from the struggle to achieve upward mobility and the cultural changes Brazil is experiencing in its development from a traditional rural to urban industrial society. So successful have been Brazil's telenovellos that they are exported to many other (mostly Spanish- or Portuguese-speaking) countries. In India, soap operas, such as *Mahabharata*, have been immensely popular and, while based on epic Hindu mythology, address modern issues of domestic conflict, particularly those concerning ownership of property. Even within a relatively cultural homogenous area such as Britain, soap operas' appeal varies according to regional cultural identity. *Emmerdale's* popularity is strongest in its native Yorkshire, like *EastEnders* in the metropolitan London area, while Welsh speakers can follow *Pobol y Cwm* (which failed to create much English interest during a subtitled season on BBC2).

Turning to one of the key global television services, MTV, on closer inspection, it is evident that it too has had to adapt its music television format in order to appeal to different national or regional audiences. In establishing MTV's European service (MTVE), there was recognition that its music programming had to reflect more pop, dance and indie music, in contrast to the hard rock, rap and metal which were prominent in its American service. Even so, European music tastes are extremely diverse, with a clear distinction between Northern Europe, with an emphasis on rock, compared to Southern Europe, with a preference for romantic ballads. MTV's music mix tends to satisfy Northern European tastes more, a factor which is reinforced by its policy of broadcasting in English. Thus in Italy, where 50 per cent of music sold is in the native language, MTV has not been popular, whereas in Germany, whose artists comprise 25 per cent of MTV's playlist, it has proved to be more successful. Nevertheless, it hasn't prevented a rival German music television service, *Viva*, from competing effectively by focusing much more strongly on German music with native German presenters. Ironically, Britain provides only a small share of the European audience because of the fact that nearly 75 per cent of households don't receive MTV.

Meanwhile, MTV's initial attempt at launching an Asian service on Hong Kong's Star TV in 1991 proved a failure, partly because of its English-speaking, North American slant. It relaunched in 1995 with a Mandarin language service, tailored more to the musical tastes of its Chinese market in Hong Kong, Taiwan and South China. A parallel English-speaking service targets other Asian markets.

Finally, with respect to the issue of global reporting of news, a recent survey of how one day's news was reported on television news across the world (Chapman, 1992) revealed marked disparities in the stories (both specific and generic) which featured in each country's television news. The report reached the following conclusion:

Figure 4.7a

If there is a headline in the news agenda survey, it is that global news coverage via satellite is an idea whose time has not yet come. The survey exposes the parochialism of news in most countries and also debunks the persistent notion that news flows from the industrialised information societies to the developing world. The story here is that news does not flow very far at all.

In all but a few instances, the news, as seen on 19 November 1991, was fiercely local. The BBC and the major American networks were exceptions, providing coverage on several regions of the world, but the much-ballyhooed CNN, on the day at least, was mostly concerned with American events. Some regions, such as Asia and Latin America, were all but invisible to outsiders, with little in the way of news reaching the rest of the world from even the most important Asian countries – for example, China, Japan and Korea.

Source: Graham Chapman, *Geographical Magazine*, October 1992.

(See Fig. 4.7b for a broad overview.)

Figure 4.7b

Broadcasting regions	Sub-Saharan Africa	L. America	N. America	W. Europe	E. Europe & USSR	Japan	China	Middle East	Other Asia	Austral-asia
Origins of news stories										
Australasia	0	0	0	0	0	4	0	0	0	56
China	0	0	0	0	1	5	64	2	3	0
W. Europe	19	4	20	63	21	0	12	43	12	20
E. Europe & USSR	5	8	10	23	80	6	14	28	12	4
Japan	0	0	0	0	3	78	10	0	2	2
Latin America	0	92	7	1	1	0	7	0	2	2
Middle East	8	2	16	19	8	0	6	17	0	0
North Africa	5	0	7	1	1	0	6	17	0	0
North America	6	7	80	11	12	1	17	13	5	14
Other Asia	2	1	1	9	0	8	21	8	80	10
Polar	0	0	0	0	0	0	0	0	0	0
Sub-Saharan Africa	80	0	9	3	0	0	7	1	1	0

Source: Intermedia, *New Agency Survey*, 1992.

Japan proved to be the most parochial in its news coverage, in contrast to France which had the best balance between national and international stories. Indeed, only one international story (about Michael Jackson's latest video) featured in Tokyo's Broadcasting news. The only conclusion which does fit the media imperialism thesis is that when news did travel across national boundaries, those stories about the developing world travelled the least.

It would seem that, despite the potential for media imperialism via new technologies like satellite television, the reality is that indigenous audiences are quite resistant to what are usually perceived as alien cultures. The recent experience of Rupert Murdoch (via his Star TV satellite service) in India is a pertinent example. Satellite television itself has rapidly gained in popularity in India but when Star TV launched in India in 1992, it only managed to attract about 2 per cent of an estimated 8 million potential viewers. A rival service, Zee TV, broadcasting in Hindi (in contrast to Star TV, broadcasting in English), quickly achieved 10 per cent of the audience. The problems of any broadcaster trying to capture an audience of up to 800 million people is that India has 18 official languages, five main religions, a complex caste system and huge disparities in wealth and education. The one audience that has shown an interest in imported satellite television is the small minority of younger, English-speaking, middle class viewers who have a more Western cultural perspective. At the other extreme are Hindu fundamentalists who have expressed strong hostility to much of the content which is perceived as morally decadent and undermining of Hindi values and beliefs.

Another example of imported Western (primarily American) television culture failing to achieve widespread popular appeal and, instead, helping to fuel anti-Western sentiment, is that of Iran between 1966 and 1979. Ali Mohammed (1990) describes how, under the Shah, Iranian National Television was used as a tool for promoting modernisation along Western lines. This included broadcasting a high (up to 78 per cent) proportion of imported television programmes, such as *Star Trek*, and *Tarzan*, together with Hollywood feature films. Much of the content of these programmes challenged traditional Iranian cultural values such as arranged marriages and the sanctity of the church, and the emphasis on consumerism was at odds with the economic opportunities available to most Iranians. Consequently, this helped to fuel resistance to the Shah, particularly from the Church, and, following his overthrow in 1979, the authorities completely rejected Western culture to the extent of banning all American television and film production.

Returning to the issue of how different audiences read or interpret media texts, one example of a television serial, *Dallas*, which has been viewed on a global scale (over 90 countries) offers further evidence of how simplistic is the notion of media imperialism. *Dallas* might be seen as a celebration of American wealth and power in its image of glamorous and opulent lifestyles and conspicuous consumption. Yet a cross-cultural study of Israeli audience responses to an episode of *Dallas* by Liebes and Katz (1990) revealed that those furthest removed from American culture (Arabs and North Africans) were inclined to see the 'message' of *Dallas* as being that 'the rich (Americans) are unhappy' and 'Americans are immoral'. Far from creating envy or material aspirations, the series proved reassuring to viewers that wealth and power involve great human cost (although Russian viewers claimed that this was what the American producers wanted audiences to believe!). *Dallas's* international success was attributed not to its particular American setting, but to its primordial narrative themes in terms of family relationships – loyalty, greed, power struggles, etc., as well as its carefully crafted narrative structure with episodic cliff-hanger and enigmatic codes.

Although the media imperialism model in its original form is now largely discredited, it would be a mistake not to recognise that there has been, and continues to be, a globalising tendency in media culture in which there is a fundamental inequality in flow from modern capitalist societies, especially America, to less developed societies, especially those labelled the 'Third World' (crude as that label may be). This has not resulted in cultural uniformity but has contributed towards new, locally adapted cultural forms, some examples of which are discussed above. What therefore needs to be examined is how the global and local interact within specific contexts in which the media are just one of many sources of cultural identity.

5 Audiences

Patterns of consumption

From a purely commercial motivation, media industries have developed quite sophisticated means of measuring the extent of media consumption by audiences. This is done primarily to justify the rates charged to advertisers who wish to target particular audiences for marketing purposes. Of particular interest is the social or demographic profile of the audience – its social class, age, gender, etc. An important consequences of this is that audiences with a less attractive social profile (for advertisers) tend to be less well served as it is simply less profitable.

For those studying the media, especially social scientists, the audience data produced by organisations like BARB (Broadcasters Audience Research Board) and RAJAR (Radio Joint Audience Research Limited) are a valuable point pf reference for examining patterns and trends in media consumption (see Figs 5.1 and 5.2 for two detailed examples).

However, such quantitative data does have its limitations. At a technical level, the methodologies for recording and measuring audience size sometimes change, giving rise to questions concerning the *reliability* of the statistics. For example, the BARB figures for television viewing used to be based on television diaries, then switched to a television meter which monitored which channels were being viewed and, finally, included handsets to ascertain which individuals in the household were actually viewing which programmes. A further refinement has been the inclusion of viewing via video recorded timeshifting after the live transmission.

A more fundamental question concerns the *validity* of the data. Do statistics concerning television viewing, radio listening and newspaper/magazine readership actually reveal the true nature of audience reception of these media? With the possible exception of cinema, where viewing conditions minimise any potential distractions, most media are received in social and physical contexts in which other activities are occurring. Thus, far from being a *primary* mode of activity, i.e. the object of close and concentrated attention, media reception is more likely to be a *secondary* mode of activity. Television viewing, for

Figure 5.1

READERSHIP OF NATIONAL DAILY NEWSPAPER (PERCENTAGE OF ADULTS) JULY–DECEMBER 1995

	Total	Male	Female	ABC1	C2DE	15–44	45+
Daily newspapers							
The Sun	22.4	25.3	19.6	14.3	30.1	26.5	17.9
Daily Mirror/Record	18.1	20.0	16.2	12.2	23.6	17.7	18.5
Daily Mail	10.1	10.5	9.6	13.3	7.0	7.9	12.4
Daily Express	6.7	7.1	6.3	8.5	4.9	5.2	8.3
The Daily Telegraph	5.6	6.4	4.8	9.9	1.5	4.3	7.0
Daily Star	4.9	6.7	3.2	2.8	6.9	6.7	2.9
The Times	3.5	4.2	2.9	6.2	1.0	3.4	3.7
The Guardian	2.5	3.1	2.0	4.4	0.7	2.9	2.2
The Independent	1.8	2.1	1.4	3.0	0.6	2.2	1.3
Financial Times	1.5	2.1	0.9	2.7	0.3	1.6	1.4

Source: National Readership Survey.

Figure 5.2

RADIO LISTENING

	% weekly reach★					Average Hours
	Adults 15+	Males	Females	ABC1	C2DE	
Radio 1	24	26	21	25	23	9.9
Radio 2	18	18	18	21	15	12.7
Radio 3	5	6	4	8	2	3.5
Radio 4	18	19	18	28	9	10.6
Radio 5	11	17	6	14	9	5.3
Classic FM	10	11	10	16	6	5.8
Virgin	9	10	7	9	9	8.3
Talk	4	5	4	5	4	6.6

★ (The number who listen to a station for a least five minutes in the course of an average week.)

Source: RAJAR *The Radio Audience* 15 January–31 March 1996.

example, is frequently undertaken alongside domestic routines such as mealtimes, household chores and family discussions. Very few people now sit down to listen attentively to the radio. Instead, it mainly functions as a background medium, qualifying in many cases as a *tertiary* mode of activity – switched on but not actively listened to.

More significantly, such quantitative data do not reveal anything about the *production of meaning*. How do audiences interpret and respond to media texts? This data can only be discovered by employing qualitative methods which are discussed later in the chapter.

Theories of the audience

The relationship between the media and their audience has been debated throughout this century. In following this debate historically, it is possible to identify phases in which there have been distinct shifts in ideas concerning the relative power of the media and the audience.

The media as 'hypodermic needle'

In the period between 1900 and the 1930s, there developed a widespread belief that the media had tremendous power in society. It was felt that society had changed from one in which social relationships were personal, intimate and communal (characterised by Ferdinand Tönnies as *gemeinschaft* society) to one in which relationships were impersonal, anonymous and isolated (*gesellschaft*). This change was thought to be caused by the twin processes of industralisation and urbanisation. The new large-scale and densely populated cities were part of a growing *mass society*. In rather pessimistic tones, individuals were now seen as part of a rootless mass, no longer belonging to a close-knit social community. The newly emergent mass media, starting with newspapers and then cinema and radio, were seen as an all-powerful means of communicating with this mass of isolated individuals. The audience was very much viewed as being acted upon by the media in a one-way process. This 'hypordermic' or (as referred to in the USA) 'magic bullet' effect was thought to be uniform and diect. Psychologically, it reflects a *behaviourist* view of learning. Media messages act as strong stimuli on the individual's emotions and sentiments, causing them to respond in a determined way, i.e. creating changes in thought and action.

These views were not based on any social scientific evidence, but on widespread speculation about the media's role in certain social changes of the time. Government propaganda during the First World War, followed by Soviet and Fascist propaganda in the 1920s and 1930s, reinforced the belief that political élites could manipulate masses through the media. Their experience of Fascist rule in Nazi Germany contributed to the Frankfurt School's critical approach toward what they saw as a mass popular culture which caused a loss of individual freedom or creative thinking and, instead, created 'false needs' (consumerism). The mass media, as part of the 'culture industry', were particularly held as responsible.

Similar conclusions, albeit from a very different academic standpoint, were reached by literary critics in Britain. In an influential text, *Mass Civilization and Minority Culture* (1930), F. R. Leavis argued that popular culture was vulgarly commercial, pandering to the lowest common tastes. The dominance of market forces (i.e. the profit motive) in culture meant that standards had fallen and civilisation was under threat. Leavis and his followers thought that an appreciation of English literature would be the only means of preserving hugh cultural standards. There followed a tradition of English teaching in schools which, at best, was suspicious of popular media products like paperback best-selling novels or TV entertainment.

This élitist view of the masses, but especially the working class, as being susceptible to power of the media still persists today. The period prior to the Second World War saw the first of many *moral panics* concerning the media's harmful influence on those viewed as most likely to be corrupted – young people. The cinema was an early target, criticised by moralist like Leavis who thought it represented the worst in popular entertainment, involving 'surrender under conditions of hypnotic receptivity to the cheapest emotional appeals' (quoted in Pearson, 1983). Apart from arousing fears of Britain becoming 'Americanised', i.e. concerned with material pleasures, vulgarity, etc., Hollywood films were accused of leading young people toward criminal behaviour through 'copycat' imitation of the villians portrayed on the screen.

This concern has, if anything, heightened during the 1980s and 1990s, leading to calls for stronger censorship of the media in order to protect vulnerable (i.e. young) audiences from possible harmful effects (see pages 124–128, for a further discussion of censorship).

From a strictly empirical point of view, no concrete research was undertaken before the 1930s to discover whether the media did cause any such effects. Mass society theorists were simply speculating about the media's influence in society.

Effects research

During the 1930s, sociologists in America began to apply their newly emergent social scientific research techniques, modelled on the natural sciences, to investigating possible media effects on audiences. The first notable example was the Payne Studies, conducted between 1929 and

1932, which undertook to discover whether films had any harmful influences on children. Their findings seemed to confirm some of the critics' fears concerning cinema – films resulted in some children suffering disturbed sleep, experiencing substantial emotional arousal and, most damningly, played a direct role in contributing towards juvenile delinquency and criminality. Soon after, in 1938, a research report (Cantril 1940) detailed how badly frightened and disturbed many people had been following just one radio programme in the USA, the *War of the Worlds*, which was presented as a 'spoof' news broadcast claiming that America had been invaded by Martians.

Although these early studies seemed to support the notion of the media being a powerful source of influence on audiences, it is now evident that the findings were either based on questionable research techniques or the results were reported in a grossly oversimplified form. In the case of the Payne Studies, the most serious claims concerning films influencing criminality were based on a mixture of interviews, including autobiographical accounts, in which the 'facts would speak for themselves' – i.e. subjects' personal recollections of how films had shaped their perceptions were considered as independent valid evidence. The fact that most of the claimed influences of films were quite benign, e.g. teaching males how to light cigarettes in a 'manly' manner, went largely unreported in the publicity surrounding the research.

On closer examination, the *War of the Worlds* research also makes a number of key points which qualify any simple conclusion concerning the power of the media. Firstly, less than one in five of the audience was in any way frightened or panicked by the broadcast. Whether or not listeners did panic was related to both personality and social factors such as education and religion. Most significantly, the radio broadcast was made much more powerful because of additional contextual factors. These included the proximity to war, the public fascination with life on other planets and, in particular, the close resemblance of the radio drama to a real news broadcast. Many listeners had strong trust in radio as a news medium – a factor that Orson Welles, the producer of *War of the Worlds*, exploited in his adaption of the novel. Unlike today, audiences then had little opportunity to cross-check the authenticity of the story on other media channels such as television.

Subsequent effects research, which has claimed to find a direct connection between exposure to media content and changes in attitude and behaviour, has often been conducted by psychologists using the laboratory method of investigation in an attempt to obtain scientific results. A prominent and influential example is the Bobo doll experiment carried out by Bandura (1965), in which children's responses to watching a film showing a child striking a Bobo doll and being either rewarded or punished were compared. Those who observed the aggression being rewarded, copied such behaviour when placed in a similar situation. While such imitative behaviour has frequently been noted in both research and everyday observations (in school playgrounds for example), it is difficult to draw any conclusions concerning personal moral development because the behaviour observed is a short-term response which is essentially playful. Children can, and do, differentiate between real and simulated violence and the resulting consequences (see the discussion below on censorship and violence).

Political effects

An alternative to the experimental psychological research has been the sociological survey. Concern about the effects of political propaganda or bias in the media led American sociologists Lazarsfeld, Berelson and Gaudet to undertake a survey in 1940 in which they tried to measure the impact of newspaper and radio political coverage of the presidential election campaign on would-be voters. They used a panel sample, whereby subjects were interviewed regularly over a six-month period leading up to the election so that the researchers could discover how the voters' radio listening or newspaper readership might shape their eventual voting decision.

When published in 1948, the *Peoples Choice* proved to be a very influential milestone in the history of effects research. The reason for this was that it demonstrated how little effect the American media had on determining electoral voting behaviour. A number of explanations were proposed.

The most significant finding was that more than half of the voters had already selected their candidate before the interviewing began. Their predisposition to vote a particular way was then reinforced through a tendency to buy only those newspapers or listen to those radio programmes which supported their views – a process of *selective exposure*. Very few were open to conversion, and those who were undecided did not show much interest in the campaign. It was also discovered that personal discussion was of much greater importance in determining political views. '*Opinion leaders*' were singled out as being especially influential. These were trusted people who were actively interested in politics and who did much to interpret media information for their immediate social group, a process the authors referred to as a *two step flow*.

The 'hypodermic' model of communication had been replaced by one that emphasised the audience as:

1 already having well-formed attitudes
2 consciously selecting and interpreting messages
3 belonging to social groups rather than being isolated individuals.

The overall conclusions seemed to be that the media's 'effect' on the audience was one of reinforcement rather than change. Instead of seeing the media as an all-powerful force working on the audience, the emerging view was that the media had only limited effects as the audience was active not passive.

However, this view has been revised to some extent in the light of a shift away from the print media as the main source of political information.

Sociologists like Jay Blumler have pointed to the increasing prominence of TV as a medium of political communication. He has argued that this has helped to 'activate' the audience politically by providing far more political information than they have ever received before. What is more, given that TV provides more 'balanced political coverage than newspapers', it has reduced the viewers' opportunity to be exposed only to those political views already held (as a Conservative supporter may be doing in buying the *Daily Express*). The overall effect, Blumler thinks, has been to make viewers more politically sceptical, and this has thus added to the growing unpredictability of voters at election time.

An additional factor which may have increased the possible influence of the media on political attitudes is the steady erosion of party loyalty. As voters have become more instrumental in their voting behaviour and less politically partisan, so they have become much readier to switch allegiance. Given that broadcasters have adhered closely to their policy of political impartiality during election campaigns, some have argued that Britain's highly partisan tabloid newspaper coverage can still be influential, especially when the result is close, even though few tabloid readers claim to trust their newspapers' political reportage. During the 1987 and 1992 elections, there was evidence that the Conservatives benefited from the strong anti-Labour bias shown in the majority of the tabloids. In the 1987 election, a Glasgow University panel sample showed the swing to the Tories among Tory tabloid readers to be 12 per cent compared to an average 5 per cent (Miller 1991). A MORI poll analysis of the 1992 election suggested that the swing to the Tories in the three months leading up to the election was highest among readers of *The Sun*

(8.5 per cent) and *The Star* (8 per cent). This was estimated to have been sufficient to account for the 1 per cent difference in voting which, essentially, decided the election, although it is certainly an exaggeration to claim that *The Sun* won the election for the Conservatives (see the headline on page 5).

When it comes to measuring longer-term political effects of the media, the methodological problems become more challenging. Not only is it difficult to attribute individual views on specific political issues to any particular media source, but it is often debatable as to what is the 'preferred reading' of media coverage of a political issue. This is especially the case for television, the most important source of political information for the majority of the population, as is made clear from the discussion of television's coverage of the miners' strike (pages 65–66). When it came to assessing audience responses to such television coverage, a similar contradiction appeared in the research conclusions (see Fig. 5.3). If researchers come to differ so significantly in their findings about the media's role in shaping public perception of one news story, then it is no surprise that the debate about the ideological effects of media representations cannot be resolved.

Figure 5.3

In a new study (Philo, 1990) groups of people from different parts of the country were given news photographs from the 1984/5 miners' strike. They were then asked to imagine that they were journalists and were invited to write their own news stories. They were also questioned about their memories of the strike and about what they believed about specific issues – for example, was the picketing that had taken place mostly peaceful or mostly violent?

One surprising result was the closeness of the 'news programmes' produced by the groups to original items which had appeared on the BBC and ITN. One year after the strike had ended, a group from Shenfield in Essex wrote the following 'news item':

'As the drift back to work in the mines began to gather momentum, violence erupted.'

A group from Glasgow pursued a similar theme:

> 'On a day that saw an increased drift back to work . . . further violence was taking place . . .

While on the original news from ITN we had heard:

> 'Worst picket violence yet but miners continue their drift back.
>
> ITN 17.45 12.11.84 . . .

It is clear that we can bring a great deal of our own history, culture and class experience to our reception of media messages. But we should not under-estimate their power and especially that of television to influence public belief. Most of the people in this study did not have direct experience of the events of the strike and did not use alternative sources of information to negotiate the dominant message on issues such as the nature of picketing. Over half of the people interviewed for our main sample believed that picketing was mostly violent. Both television and the press were given as key sources of information but people spoke of the special power of television, saying that its images were 'more immediate' and 'stuck more'. As one resident of Glasgow put it, 'Seeing is believing.'

Source: G. Philo, 'Seeing is Believing', *Social Studies Review,* May 1991.

During the miners' strike I, with three colleagues, carried out (with NOP) two national sample surveys which help explain their curious reactions to the dispute. This week we published a research study, *Television and the Miners' Strike,* based on the results.

We found that during the strike – at least from August 1984 to March 1985 – sympathy towards the miners increased. In particular, among Conservatives the numbers saying they were 'not at all sympathetic to the miners strike' declined from 52 per cent to 38 per cent . . .

There was very little correspondence between the issues identified by the public as important and the proportion or pattern of coverage they received in the news (at least as given by our content analysis of the major television news bulletins). Thus 'who rules the country?' very rarely appeared as an issue on television (at less than 1 per cent on our issue count), while the economics of coal production/pit closures/unemployment amounted to only

3.7 per cent. Picketing violence was an issue of major importance, but it declined in importance both on the news and in public perception. Ballots were in the news mainly in the first two months of the strike (where they received half their total television news coverage) but remained important in public perceptions.

It is very difficult to reconcile our results with theories that television 'sets the agenda' of issues for the public. Certainly there is little correspondence between the frequency with which issues were covered in the news and their perceived importance by the public.

Source: G. Cumberbatch, 'How the miners really lost', *New Society*, 23 May 1986.

However, it must be said that most researchers now recognise the *active* role of the audience in selecting and interpreting the media according to differing social and cultural contexts. Following the first wave of effects research in the 1940s and 1950s, attention turned to how audiences actively use the media in order to fulfil certain needs.

Uses and gratifications

There is now quite a long history of studies detailing the appeals of media consumption for the audience. Blumler and Katz's research (1974) is typical of the uses and gratifications approach. They attempted to discover the goals of TV viewing from the viewers themselves. During unstructured group discussions they listed the main motives for viewing as suggested by respondents, then compiled a list of the most frequently mentioned statements and submitted this to a cross-section of TV viewers to discover the main uses and gratifications categories.

The needs which TV most satisfied were found to be:

1 *diversion* – forms of escape or emotional release from everyday pressures
2 *personal relationships* – companionship for lonely people, or a source of conversation
3 *personal identity* – being able to compare one's life with the programme content, exploring personal problems and reinforcing personally held values

4 *surveillance* – source of information about the world.

(See Fig. 5.4 for a uses and gratifications analysis of TV quiz shows.)

Figure 5.4   Uses and gratifications of TV quiz programmes

Cluster 1 Self-rating appeal
I can compare myself with the
   experts
I like to imagine that I am on
   the programme and doing well
I feel pleased that the side I
   favour has actually won
I imagine that I was on the
   programme and doing well
I am reminded of when I was in
   school
I laugh at the contestant's
   mistakes
Hard to follow

Cluster 2 Basis for social interaction
I look forward to talking about it
   with others
I like competing with other
   people watching with me
I like working together with the
   family on the answers
I hope the children will get a lot
   out of it
The children get a lot out of it
It brings the family together
   sharing the same interest
It is a topic of conversation
   afterwards
Not really for people like myself

Cluster 3 Excitement appeal
I like the excitement of a close
   finish

I like to forget my worries for a
   while
I like trying to guess the winner
Having got the answer right I
   feel really good
I completely forget my worries
I get involved in the competition
Exciting

Cluster 4 Educational appeal
I find I know more than I
   thought
I feel I have improved myself
I feel respect for the people on
   the programme
I think over some of the
   questions afterwards
Educational

Cluster 5
It is nice to see the experts
   taken down a peg
It is amusing to see the mistakes
some of the contestants make

Cluster 6
I like to learn something as well
   as to be entertained
I like finding out new things

Cluster 7
I like trying to guess the answers
I hope to find that I know some
   of the answers

Cluster 8
I find out the gaps in what I
    know
I learn something new
A waste of time

Cluster 9
Entertaining
Something for all the family

Cluster 10
I like the sound of voices in the
    house
I like seeing really intelligent
    contestants showing how
    much they know

Source: D. McQuail, J. Blumler and J. Brown, 'The television audience: a
revised perspective', in *McQuail*, 1972.

In taking audience goals and orientation as the starting point for
research, uses and gratifications can be placed within the *interpretive*
perspective. No assumption is made about how media content affects the
audience, nor is this attempted. Indeed, the strategy is not far removed
from market research undertaken by media organisations seeking to
discover their audience and where needs are not being met. As such, it
also fits into a pluralist view of the media – supply meets demand, the
consumer selects the desired product from the media supermarket shelf.
It is clear that many TV programmes, newspapers, magazines, etc., appeal
to distinct social groups.

Criticisms

By suggesting that individuals have certain 'needs', the theory comes
very close to a kind of 'psychological functionalism', i.e. the media exist
to meet those universal needs. However, critics have posed the following
related questions:

1 Are not those 'needs' to some extent determined by learning to enjoy
   or make use of what is available, i.e. a choice ultimately made not by
   the audience but by media producers? Supply shapes demand.
2 Can it be taken for granted that the audience is aware of the pleasures
   inherent in media representations? Psychologists influenced by the
   work of Freud have suggested that media images and symbols may
   appeal to an individual's *unconscious desires* which have been repressed
   since childhood. This particularly applies to sexuality in the various
   forms in which it is expressed in films, magazines, etc.
3 Are these uses and gratifications individual needs or social/subcultural
   group needs? If the latter, then it becomes much more problematic as
   to how different social groups may make use of the same content.

Media or audience power – the swinging pendulum

By the late 1960s, media sociologists were working with very different ideas about the audience. They had more modest expectations regarding the discovery of any 'effects'; the audience was now seen as active not passive; and the long-term effects of ideological content were being appraised.

However, this did not stop a reassertion of the primacy of the media in terms of their influence over audiences:

'it can be argued that the basic reason behind the shift in the argument about the effects from a powerful to a limited to a more powerful mode is that the social world was being transformed over this period . . . Powerful effects of communication were sensed in the thirties because the Depression and the political current surrounding the war had created a fertile seed for the production of certain kinds of effects. Similarly, the normalcy of the fifties and sixties led to a limited effects model. In the late sixties a period of war, political discord and inflation combined to expose the social structure in fundamental ways and to make it permeable by the media of communication.'

Source: J. Carey quoted in *McQuail*, 1983.

It has been argued that such social change has contributed to a combination of more *audience dependency* on the media for information and an attempt by those with power to use the media as a social control and influence. Television, in particular, has seemed to become more significant as a source of knowledge, given the way social institutions like government, education and religion have tried to gain access to the airwaves.

One American writer who has argued that TV has become more important as a source of information on social reality is George Gerbner. In a kind of 'mass society mark 2 model', he proposed that the audience has become increasingly isolated and reliant on TV for information about the outside world. As such, TV has a *cultivation effect*, i.e. shaping beliefs and consciousness of social reality. By using content analysis, Gerbner has shown how TV 'distorts' reality, especially in portraying the world as a violent place. He has followed this up with an audience survey in which he has shown that 'heavy' viewers (who watch an above average amount of TV) are much more likely to overestimate the real amount of violence in society (i.e. as revealed in official statistics) – an effect he calls the 'cultivation differential'. However, it is not clear whether television has created these beliefs or simply reinforced them.

Coming from very different academic (and largely French) origins, but still privileging the power of the media, were structuralist writers, such as Althusser, Levi Strauss and Lacan, who blended structuralism with Marxism, anthropology and psychoanalysis, respectively. Their writings are too complex to summarise here but, essentially, they argued that media texts contain structured patterns – of narrative form, political ideology, sexual voyeurism, etc. – which position audiences and determine the kinds of pleasures and meanings that will be produced.

Ironically, structuralism's emphasis on the textual coding of meaning, especially within semiology, allowed subsequent (post structuralist) writers to shift the emphasis away from the power of the text towards the power of the *reader* or audience. This was because, once the *polysemic* nature of signs and texts was acknowledged, that allowed space for different patterns of audience interpretation or *decoding*.

In Britain, the Centre for Contemporary Cultural Studies (CCCS) has also considered the question of how audiences make sense of, or *decode*, media output within their various social contexts. Borrowing from semiology, Stuart Hall has suggested that media forms (or texts) are encoded ideologically with a *preferred meaning* to be understood by the audience, but that there is a degree of freedom for various audience decodings or interpretations of the text content (the signs). These decodings may be related to specific social situations. For example, among the working class, they might range from complete acceptance of the dominant ideology contained in a TV programme to a rejection, or oppositional decoding, of the programme. The acceptance might be found within affluent, privatised, working class areas, whereas the oppositional reading might come from the more traditional 'proletarian' working class areas, especially among committed trade unionists (although in the last 20 years such areas have dramatically declined).

To test this idea, David Morley (1980), interviewed various social groups about their responses to *Nationwide*, the BBC's weekday current affairs magazine of the 1970s. Groups tending towards a dominant reading (i.e. those seen by Morley as closest to *Nationwide*'s own values) included bank managers and apprentices, while those rejecting *Nationwide* and producing an oppositional reading included black further education students and shop stewards. In between (having a 'negotiated' reading) were teacher training and university students and trade union officials. By interviewing groups of viewers, Morley did not fall into the trap of seeing the TV audience as composed of isolated individuals.

The 1980s saw a stream of studies which revealed how audiences' readings of media texts varied according to different social and cultural factors. Some argued that audiences were empowered by their ability to actively produce their own distinctive meanings and pleasures, especially in relation to specific media genres which require particular *cultural competences* available to such audiences. For example, writers like Charlotte Brunsdon (1987) have suggested that women are more competent at reading soap operas because this requires more feminine skills – 'sensitivity, perception, intuition and the concerns of personal life which are called on and practised in the genre'. Because soaps are based in the sphere of the personal and domestic, women are more familiar with, and responsive to, the narrative. The fact that many men denigrate soaps only serves to provoke female viewers to identify more strongly with the genre as a symbol of cultural resistance and independence.

A more surprising example of how soap opera provides opportunities for developing cultural identities is described by Marie Gillespie (1995) in her study of how young South Asians living in London use television in their daily lives. The most popular television programme of the Asians in her survey was *Neighbours* (see Fig. 5.5). The popularity of *Neighbours* with Asians might be unexpected in that some commentators have criticised it and its 'sister' soap *Home and Away* for being implicitly racist through a failure to include any significant ethnic minorities as the main characters. This is further evidence of how misleading it might be simply to read off the 'preferred meaning' of media texts without recourse to investigating different cultural interpretations of such texts. In extreme cases, some audiences may even appropriate media characters so that they become expressive signifiers of their own cultural identity. In America, *The Simpsons*, a cartoon series featuring a working class white family, proved extremely popular among black children and teenagers. Bart Simpson, the teenage anti-hero, captured the street style and attitude of black youth culture and, before long, black Bart Simpson images started appearing on teeshirts, in graffiti, etc.

One area of the media which has intermittently been a vehicle for symbolic cultural 'resistance' is pop music. From folk 'protest' music and hippie counterculture in the 1960s, to punk in the 1970s, through to hip hop and rap music in the 1980s/90s, the music has been centripetal to distinctive youth subcultures. Some sociologists (see for example, S. Hall and T. Jefferson, 1976) have claimed that these subcultures have functioned as a form of opposition to hegemonic social groups, be they

Figure 5.5
Talk about soaps – in particular *Neighbours*, much the most popular TV programme at the time of fieldwork – reveals critical views of the social and cultural characteristics of Southall as a 'neighbourhood' and a 'community'. It often leads on to comparative and contrasting reflections about the place of 'gossip' in local life, about patterns of kinship and gender relations, about courtship and marriage and about intergenerational conflict about these subjects. Soap talk often functions as a surrogate for talk about personal and family concerns which cannot be directly voiced. It also often concerns what are perceived as positive aspects of the social life represented in *Neighbours* – in particular the freedoms enjoyed by young people in the soap, notably in the field of gender relations and in the unconstrained communication between people of all generations. Young people contrast these representations with their experience of local and domestic life. But the deeper reasons for the enormous popularity of *Neighbours* lie elsewhere. It is due to a homology which young people perceive, between a feature of the social relations depicted in *Neighbours* and a feature of social relations in the adult world of Southall, which they intensely resent: the centrality of gossip as a medium of information and control, especially the social control of gender relations. As my analysis shows, this homology can be extended: in important respects, the form of narration which characterises soaps, and the form of their collaborative reception in talk, both resemble gossip and rumour as processes of collective narration. And gossip – especially about gender relations – is of course also an essential feature of young people's everyday communication, as they freely admit. The term 'gossip' is, then, the linchpin which articulates the relationship between soap, soap talk, social experience and social interaction in the peer group and in the social environment which they inhabit.
        Source: M. Gillespie, *Television Ethnicity and Cultural Change*, 1995.

based on class, generation or race (see the discussion of rap on pages 74–75).

Although it is important to recognise the openness or polysemic nature of many media texts and the range of cultural interpretations or readings that are produced by different audiences, there is a danger that the freedom and 'power' of audiences may be exaggerated. This has tended to be the case with those who claim we now live in a postmodern society in which cultural identities are a matter of individuals choosing from the rich range on offer in the media. This position can easily slip into an uncritical celebration of popular culture and a romanticisation of cultural resistance and opposition wherever this can be identified. In so doing, what tends to be ignored are two key constraints arising from real social structural inequalities:

1 the material context in which people exist – their economic power and life chances in terms of employment, education, etc.
2 the production context in which media texts are made – the limited ownership of, and access to, media production.

These structural realities are a vital influence in shaping both what media production is made available to audiences and the nature of their response.

Approaches to audience research

The main challenge to discovering how audiences respond to the media is in choosing and applying a suitable research methodology. Theoretical and practical issues need to be considered. Those researchers who are guided by a desire to be scientific and who seek quantitative data which can underpin causal explanations of the relationship between the media and audiences, tend towards very structured methodologies. These might be labelled positivistic. In contrast, other researchers prefer to produce qualitative data which reveal meanings and audience perceptions of the media. These might be labelled ethnographic. However, this is a crude and oversimplified distinction. Researchers often integrate different methods and seek to blend a mix of quantitative and qualitative data in a process of triangulation.

The most structured form of audience research is the *experiment* in which an experimental group is subject to some media stimulus and their behaviour or attitudinal response is measured and compared to a control group who are not subject to the same media stimulus. An example of experimental research is Bandura (1965), described above. The main advantage of this approach is that any audience responses observed can be more directly attributed to the media stimulus than could be inferred from more naturalistic settings in which other possible determining variables may be at work, e.g. the peer group, home, etc. Conversely, however, experiments, especially those conducted in laboratories, are artificial, and it is questionable how far subjects' behaviour can be applied to the 'real' world. It has been suggested that subjects often provide the responses they think the experimenter is seeking, the so called 'experimenter demand effect'. A further problem is that the media stimuli provided, such as films or television programmes, tend to be selected according to the experimenter's interests and are usually viewed in very contrived conditions. In other words, the research fails to allow for the social context in which audiences normally receive the media. Finally, experimental research is very much confined to assessing short-term behavioural effects without addressing the issue of mental processes – what meanings and ideas do audiences produce from media texts?

Going beyond behavioural responses, while still retaining a quantitative and controlled design, is the *survey*. An alternative to the experiment, which still retains an emphasis on cause and effect, is the *longitudinal survey* or *panel study*. Here the aim is to investigate possible relationships between media content and audiences over a period of time, and this has the advantage of identifying longer-term cumulative media influences. A pioneering example is the voting study by Lazerfeld et al. (1948), discussed above. Working in reverse is a survey by Belson (1978) in which a sample of teenage boys were asked about their media consumption and attitudes towards violence at different points in their past life in order to see whether television viewing might have contributed towards their violent behaviour. However, retrospective accounts of media consumption must be considered problematic in terms of memory lapses, and any relationship to violent behaviour established cannot be proven as causal because the precise sequencing of viewing and violent behaviour is not known. Even the most exhaustive longitudinal survey cannot sustain many opportunities to interrogate media usage and parallel social behaviour to determine how the two interact.

Surveys are best at producing a snapshot, or cross-sectional, account of patterns of media consumption and associated attitudes and beliefs according to different social profiles. A good example of such a survey is that carried out by the Policy Studies Institute (PSI) in 1993, in which 78 juvenile offenders, aged 12–18, were interviewed about their media consumption and compared to 538 schoolchildren of a similar age. The main purpose was to discover whether the offenders shared a distinctively different pattern of media consumption, particularly with respect to violence. The schoolchildren were given a confidential questionnaire to complete, and the young offenders were asked the same questions by interviewers.

One concern about self-report surveys like this one is the potential to misrepresent actual media consumption. For example, the researchers could not cross-check actual television viewing behaviour. Allowing for this, the survey was able to reveal certain patterns which could be used as evidence to refute the widely held assumption that young violent offenders share an abnormally high preference for violent films, television programmes and video games (see the discussion on censorship below). The main limitation of this research, as acknowledged by the author, is that the quantitative data produced are largely descriptive. Most of the questions asked are closed, with little scope for subjects to articulate their own personal ideas or perceptions. When the PSI researchers tried to discover reasons for the offenders' media choices, the responses seemed rather superficial. Describing one typical offender's response they report:

> 'His three favourite films were *Terminator 2, Full Metal Jacket* and *Predator*. The first two have been covered, the third was seen on video, thirty times. If he could be anyone on television, it would be (predictably) Arnold Schwarzenegger, because "he's just right for the stuff he does". He also likes Jean Claude Van Damme, "just because I enjoy his films".

Audience researchers, particularly in the sociology and cultural studies disciplines, have tended to favour qualitative research methods as a means of discovering how audiences interpret and experience media texts. The core strategy is to facilitate responses which are a valid expression of subjective meanings – allowing people to speak in their own terms. One approach is the *in-depth interview* where the researcher applies a flexible agenda incorporating open-ended questions which will give individuals the freedom to express their genuine feelings and ideas about a subject. This necessarily places greater demands on the researcher in terms of interviewing skills – gaining the subject's confidence, knowing when to intervene and probe, etc. A further problem is being able to examine and interpret the detailed verbal responses so that some kind of descriptive and/or explanatory commentary can be provided rather than merely a series of quotes interspersed with questions. Naturally, there is scope here for the researcher's own prejudices to help to shape the account that emerges. David Buckingham's description (see Fig. 5.6) of his small group discussions with young people concerning *EastEnders* is a good example of one variation of the open-ended interview.

Buckingham admits that the fact that the discussions occurred in a school environment, and that he was a guest teacher figure, meant that the children's responses might not be totally authentic. To overcome this hurdle the researcher needs to adopt an *ethnographic* approach to studying the audience. This means, as far as possible, immersing yourself in the lives of your subjects to such an extent that you can reconstruct the meaning (of the media) from the subject's own perspective. Within the social sciences, the approach was developed in its purest form in the participant observation research used by social anthropologists when trying to understand the lives of alien cultures. It is a method which requires commitment to a lengthy period of fieldwork and being fully accepted by the cultural group under investigation. Clearly, this has particular advantages when such a group shares a (sub) culture which is not well understood and frequently misrepresented, as is the case with many minority groups in British society.

One such minority group are South Asians who feature in Marie Gillespie's ethnographic study discussed above. In describing her fieldwork she identifies three key stages: groundwork, immersion and focusing. Groundwork refers to her initial research and entry into the culture – facilitated by teaching English and media studies in a local high school. Immersion, the most intensive phase, lasted two years and involved keeping verbatim transcripts of conversations and interviews to build up field notes, while also participating in the peer and family cultures of the young Asians (Gillespie is white) and watching the same popular television programmes and films. Finally, focusing involved applying more purposive methods designed to pursue a more clearly defined research agenda. Particularly valuable here were informal group discussions arising from her media studies teaching. The net result is an account which includes 'verbatim accounts of informants in order to let young people's voices speak as much as possible to bear witness to their experiences and perceptions and also to open up the text for further interpretation.' (For an insight into the value of an ethnographic approach relative to the survey, Fig. 5.8.)

Nevertheless, even with this form of ethnographic research, there are limits to the nature of the participant observation possible. Because television viewing is situated largely within a domestic setting, it is difficult to access the immediate context of reception without significantly changing the natural environment. One solution to this,

Figure 5.6

My intention was to make these discussions as open-ended as possible, and to avoid directing them towards particular issues. I began each session by asking some fairly basic questions about viewing habits: when and why had they started to watch the programme, how many times a week did they see it, did other members of their family watch it, and so on. I would then ask each member of the group to identify their favourite, and their least favourite, characters, and to give reasons for their choices. This question was normally sufficient to guarantee animated discussion for the remainder of the time available; my only subsequent questions were to clarify points of confusion, and occasionally to draw out more reticent members of the group.

Sometimes, generally towards the end of the discussion, I would draw the group's attention to characters or stories which they had failed to mention, at least partly to discover if there were reasons for this. Finally, usually for about the last twenty minutes of the session, I would screen a videotape of *EastEnders*, occasionally pausing the tape to invite comments from the group.

By adopting this relatively self-effacing role, I was attempting to allow the group to define its own agenda for discussion. What the groups chose to talk about, and what they chose to ignore, were in themselves significant. Furthermore, by intervening as little as possible, and encouraging the group members to interact directly with each other, rather than through a 'mediator', I was aiming to identify more accurately *how* they would discuss the programme in their everyday conversation.

Source: David Buckingham, *Public Secrets: EastEnders and its Audience*, 1987.

pioneered by Peter Collett (1986), is to install cameras alongside the domestic video-recorder to film people watching television. This method is an example of pure *observation* as a research tool and is valuable as a means of recording the variety of social and personal activity audiences undertake while 'viewing' television.

However, as a means of revealing the meanings audiences derive from television, it is confined to random spontaneous verbal responses provoked by specific programmes.

By itself, any individual research method is unlikely to reveal answers to the range of questions posed by media researchers. Each method has its own strengths and weaknesses, and its suitability will largely depend on the specific nature of the research issues being addressed as well as the researcher's own theoretical assumptions. The overriding danger is that insufficient attention is paid to the *context*, be that social, political, economic or historical, in which media audiences exist. As an example of the significance of these contexts in shaping debates about media audiences, let us consider the issue of censorship.

Censorship

Censorship refers to the blocking, manipulating and regulating of media content. No society has complete freedom to produce and circulate media texts regardless of content. The two principal motives for censorship are political and moral. Political censorship arises from concerns about national security and political consensus, and is discussed in Chapter 3. Moral censorship exists because of a perceived need to uphold certain accepted minimum standards concerning moral codes, without which serious anti-social behaviour would flourish. The greatest concern tends to be expressed about violent and sexual representations, although blasphemy and bad language are also included as areas of likely offence.

Like all other countries with well-developed media institutions, Britain has a range of regulatory constraints which restrict what is legally acceptable to make available to different age groups, e.g. the British Board of Film Classification (BBFC) system of certifying films U, PG, 18, etc. With respect to sexual content, the Obscene Publications Act covers all the media and states that it is an offence to include any material that is likely to deprave or corrupt audiences. Whether or not these regulations are sufficient is a matter of controversy. It is possible to identify two polemical positions at opposite ends of the debating spectrum. Those who feel censorship is necessary and should be strengthened can be called *moralists*. Their main complaint is that standards of social responsibility have been falling in the media, allowing unacceptable media representations to appear, particularly relating to violence and sex. The opposition stance, emanating from a *libertarian* position, is that individuals should have the freedom to decide for themselves whether any media content is acceptable, and that it is undesirable and potentially dangerous to allow any organisation or third party to control access to media texts. In examining the key issues in this debate, the spotlight will be focused on the two most contentious forms of representation, violence and pornography (which itself can frequently be based on violence).

What effects?

Speculation about possible media affects on audiences has tended to emphasise the harmful influences that can accrue from violent and pornographic content. Among the numerous suggested effects, the following have been prominent:

1   *Social learning* – the key notion here is that the media supply role models for audiences, especially children, to identify with and imitate. Such was the assumption underlying Bandura's Bobo doll experiments (see pages 107–108).
2   *Instigation* – here there is an assertion that media representations stimulate or arouse a strong emotional reaction which may, in turn, trigger excitement and subsequent aggression.
3   *Desensitisation* – this refers to the decreasing impact arising from repeated representations of nominally disturbing or shocking images. Over time, audiences thus become tolerant, and even accepting, of anti-social representations, e.g. sadistic acts of violence or rape.
4   *Catharsis* – in contrast to the above, this theory suggests that media representations may actually reduce anti-social behaviour because audiences are able to release their emotions through experiencing or participating vicariously in the actions of characters in media narratives. This is often cited in the defence of pornography as a means of satiating frustrated sexual urges.

This list does not exhaust the range of suggested effects. For example, some have claimed that audiences who depend heavily on the media for information about contemporary society are more likely to develop exaggerated fears about the risks of being a victim of violent crime (see Gerbner and Gross, 1976). A real problem in discussing possible effects is the need to distinguish between short-term *behavioural* effects, such as experiencing an immediate arousal, and the long-term *ideological* effects, such as an acceptance of the legitimacy of some groups' use of violence in certain contexts. A good example of this is the argument made by many feminists that pornography is a form of misogyny in so far as it celebrates the representation of patriarchal power and the exploitation of women (see Fig. 5.7).

Figure 5.7

What is Pornography

Pornography is about power – men's power over women. In it we are seen as vulnerable, helpless, open, submissive and longing to be violated. However the woman is portrayed in porn, whether as enjoying or resisting, the purpose is to give men pleasure and to increase their power over us . . .

The images of women portrayed in pornography are a true representation of what men think female sexuality is. We like to be 'man-handled', raped, abused: we are shown to be masochistic, that is enjoying pleasure through pain, whilst men derive pleasure through inflicting pain. Pornography shows this very clearly.

Source: Women Against Violence Against Women.

I don't think that pornography is in and of itself violence against women, or incitement to sexual hatred. No representations have intrinsic meaning: a representation of a naked woman or a woman having sex doesn't have an intrinsic meaning. In a totally different culture, where nakedness and sex had different connotations, the meanings of such representations could be quite other. Meaning is given to a representation by its context, use and the arrangement of elements in it. The meanings of an image are decided by how it is lit, framed, the position of the subject, where her look is directed, and so on. Feminists, and women in general, tend to find offensive the *form* in which sexuality is shown in pornography.

Source: Rosalind Coward, *Spare Rib* No 119, June 1982.

Source: 'What is Pornography?' R. Betterton, *Looking On*, Pandora, 1987.

The evidence

Given the difficulties there are in demonstrating any cause and effect relationship between media stimuli and audience responses within the short term (see the discussion about Bandura's Bobo doll experiment above), it is not surprising that long-term effects are impossible to prove. Nevertheless, there have been literally hundreds of research projects concerning violence, pornography and the media over the years. As such, it is possible to discover evidence to support virtually any theoretical stance adopted.

The largest amount of publicity has surrounded so called 'celebrity' cases where notorious criminals' media usage has been the focus of attention. This has usually been connected to ongoing moral panics concerning the level of violence in the media, discussed below. Politicians and the tabloid press have connected particularly shocking crimes and specific films, such as the James Bulger murder in 1992 (linked to *Child's Play 3*), and the Hungerford massacre in 1987 (linked to *Rambo: First Blood: Part 2*). This has reinforced suspicions of a direct causal effect, despite the links in these cases being tenuous or non-existent. Even where murderers or rapists have been found to enjoy violent or pornographic films, there is no clear evidence that these were a determining factor in their criminal behaviour. Criminals often look for an explanatory rationale which may be used in court as a mitigating defence strategy.

Most of the evidence which purports to demonstrate a direct causal connection between the media and violent behaviour is based on experimental (especially laboratory-based) research, the limitations of which are discussed above. Two particular investigations which have cast doubt about direct effects are based on correlation survey techniques. Kutchinsky (1990) conducted a cross-cultural survey in which he examined the impact of a liberalising of the pornography legislation on sexual crime in Denmark, Sweden and Germany, and found an actual decrease in such crime. The incidence of rape decreased as access to pornography became easier. Needless to say, anti-pornographers claimed other factors were responsible, such as changes in police recording of sexual crime.

In Britain the PSI survey of 1993 (described on pages 120–121) found that the television and film preferences of juvenile offenders were virtually indistinguishable from those of the schoolchildren. Both groups enjoyed mainstream texts such as *EastEnders*, *Neighbours* and *The Bill*. In fact, a larger proportion of the offenders than of the schoolchildren reported watching no television at all. The favourite film for both groups was *Terminator 2*.

In discussing media effects, it needs to be emphasised that much depends on the kind of theoretical assumptions researchers hold about the nature of media audiences. There is a tendency for those who claim direct and powerful effects to assume that audiences are relatively passive and vulnerable to influence, especially children. In contrast, more sceptical researchers tend to start with the premise that audiences are active in their use and interpretation of the media. That is not to say that no harmful effects may arise, but that audience pleasures need to be recognised in what is often a complex relationship between text and audience. For example, David Buckingham (1994), investigating children's responses to horror films, describes how such films simultaneously delight and distress young viewers often in very unpredictable ways. In the case of pornography, the texts can be seen as an opportunity for audiences simply to fantasise about sexual desires which may be repressed in 'respectable' society (see Gibson and Gibson, 1993). How different audiences respond to violence and pornography in the media will, to some extent, be shaped by the cultural contexts in which such audiences select and interpret particular texts. Hence the value of employing an ethnographic approach (see Fig. 5.8).

Textual meanings

In debating the harm or otherwise of media texts containing violence and pornography, a fundamental issue concerns how far it is possible to categorise or classify what constitutes acceptable or unacceptable representations. There are no shortage of working definitions, which include the following:

> 'A work is likely to be regarded as obscene if it portrays violence to such a degree and so explicitly that its appeal can only be to those who are disposed to desire positive enjoyment from seeing such violence.'
>
> *Source*: Richard Falcon, *Classified*, 1994.

> 'Pornography refers to a set of images aimed at sexual arousal which are offensive to reasonable people.'
> *Source*: The Williams Report on Obscenity and Film Censorship, 1979.

> 'Sexually degrading means the depiction of women as willing recipients of any male sexual urge or as oversexed, highly promiscuous individuals with insatiable sexual urges.'
> *Source*: E. Donnerstein et al. 1987.

Terms like obscene, offensive, degrading, etc., are evaluative and relative to different people and historical contexts (see the debate over definitions of pornography in Fig. 5.8). Within contemporary Europe, for example, there are clearly significant variations in the degree to which sexually explicit representations are acceptable between different countries. Historically, there has been a dramatic shift in attitudes towards

Figure 5.8
Views from the boys: ethnographic perspectives
Dr Belson is not alone in concentrating on teenage boys. They have also been the main focus of most of the ethnographic studies of delinquency. The past couple of years or so have produced several notable contributions to this genre, including Howard Parker and Owen Gill on Liverpool, Paul Willis on Wolverhampton, and Dave Robins and Phil Cohen on the East End. Although they cover some of the same ground as Belson, they approach it very differently. Where Belson opts for a large cross-sectional sample from all over London, they opt for intensive studies of particular groups of working-class boys in specific localities. Where Belson uses interviews and self-report schedules, they rely on observations of actual behaviour coupled with repeated conversations and informal interviews over a period of months, sometimes years. Where Belson aims to establish a link between high exposure to violent television programmes and high involvement in acts of violence, they set out to explore the ways in which acts of violence and other forms of delinquency arise out of specific social situations and sets of relations, and are underpinned by particular meanings drawn from wider class and neighbourhood cultures . . .

The ethnographic evidence points to a strong connection between involvement in violence (particularly vandalism and fighting) and immersion in the male street culture rooted in the working-class neighbourhood. It also indicates that the impact of televised violence is relatively marginal. This does not mean that television has no impact, but it does suggest (1) that it is a subsidiary factor and (2) that its effects are mediated through the pre-existing situational cultures.

Source: G. Murdoch and R. McCron, 'The Broadcasting and Delinquency Debate', Screen Education, Spring 1979.

representations of violence and sexuality since the Second World War. For example, in 1953, the British Board of Film Censors banned *The Wild One* because of its treatment of American gang violence. The film was eventually granted a licence in 1966 and the uncensored version can now be seen on daytime television.

In deciding on whether or not to censor media texts containing violent and sexual representations, regulatory bodies like the BBFC have to try to reflect (mythical) consensual moral standards. What makes such work very challenging is the need to consider the *textual context* within which any representations appear.

To try simply to identify a list of unacceptable forms of representation or even quantify a permissible limit for the number of such representations is not a means by which censorship can effectively be applied. It all depends on the justification for including particular representations and what kind of audience may be involved. Acts of violence appear in a large variety of media contexts – everything from television news to cartoons to soap opera. These contain different modalities of realism and audiences thus adjust their expectations and judgements accordingly. For example, it has been found that British television viewers are far more likely to be disturbed by violence in crime drama set in Britain than in America, especially when committed by men against women (Gunter, 1985).

Whatever the intentions of those producing media texts, it is often uncertain as to how these will be interpreted by different audiences. Few depictions of rape go uncensored in Britain for fear of offering voyeuristic pleasure to male viewers. A film that set out to examine the issues of guilt and violence surrounding rape, *The Accused*, divided critics due to the range of audience viewing positions made available in the filming of the rape scene. In a study of female responses by Schlesinger et al. (1992), it was found that women who themselves had experienced sexual violence were inclined to identify with the victim and blame all the male participants, while some women reported that male friends were inclined to blame the victim for bringing the rape on herself by her behaviour, and the women were also concerned that the rape scene did permit male sexual gratification.

The more that media texts move away from simple generic formulae, with clearly identified moral positions, and engage in irony, parody and morally ambiguous narratives (as is typical of postmodernism), the more difficult it becomes to make confident judgements about the rationale for censoring such texts. Audiences, too, are more pluralistic in their cultural values and judgements, so that an increasing number of decisions taken by censors are called into question.

Whose concern?

During the past decade there has been a steady stream of well-publicised comments and debates concerning the issue of violence and sex in the media. Most of the pressure has been applied towards a tightening of the regulations governing the censorship of violence and sex in the media and this has frequently been inspired by individual cases, such as the James Bulger murder case, which, in turn, have created mini moral panics.

Despite these panics, several surveys have found little evidence of a growth in public concern. For example, an Independent Television Commission survey in 1993 found that only one in ten viewers had been offended by violence and/or sex on television. In its annual survey of viewer's attitudes in 1995, 58 per cent of terrestrial viewers felt that people should be allowed to subscribe to violent or pornographic channels (this figure rose to 75 per cent for cable and satellite viewers).

There is little doubt that campaigns for increased censorship of the media are associated with changes in the political landscape and the relative success of different groups in shaping the moral agenda via the media. In America, the rise of the new right (the so called 'moral majority') has been instrumental in the introduction of new controls which have extended to the 'V chip' technology, providing increased parental control of children's television viewing. In the case of pornography, the new right have found an unlikely ally among radical feminists who think pornography is a form of partriarchal oppression.

For mainstream politicians, the media have proved to be a convenient scapegoat in the search for simple explanations and solutions to complex social problems, especially in relation to the behaviour of young people. However, as any historian of moral panics concerning youth and popular entertainment would reveal, with each new moral panic there is a consistent tendency to imagine a golden age in which young people were uncorrupted by exposure to the evils of popular culture, be that films, comics, pop music, television, video nasties or computer video games. Consider the following commentary concerning the popularity of comic books in America during the late 1940s and early 1950s. A major critic of these comics was a psychiatrist, Dr Louis Wertham, and his critique was published in 1954 under the title *The Seduction of the Innocent*.

'While crime comics were certainly not the only cause of delinquency, Wertham believed them to be a major one in many cases, particularly cases involving serious delinquencies. Up to the beginning of the comic book era, he reasoned, there were hardly any serious crimes, such as murder, committed by children under twelve years of age. Yet, in the 1950s he saw younger and younger children committing more and more serious and violent crimes. Indeed, in 1953, *The New York Times* commented in an editorial, "It is difficult to think of children as burglars, gangsters, drug addicts, or murderers. Such has become the reality, however." '

Source: S. Lowery et al., *Milestones in Mass Communication Research*, 1988.

References

Ali Mohammadi, 'Cultural Imperialism and Cultural Identity' in Downing J. et al *Questioning the Media*, Sage, 1990.

Anderson, D. and Sherrock, W. 'Biasing the News: Technical issues in Media Studies', *British Journal of Sociology*, 13 (3), 1979.

Bandura, A., 'Vicarious processes: a case of no-trial learning' in Berkowitz, L. ed. *Advances in Experimental Social Psychology*, Vol. 2, Academic Press, 1963.

Barry A., 'Black Mythologies: representations of black people on British Television' in Twitchin, J., *The Black and White Media Show Book*, Trentham Books, 1988.

Becker, H., *The Outsiders*, Free Press, 1963.

Belson, W., *Television Violence and the Adolescent Boy*, Saxon House, 1978.

Boyd-Barrett, O., 'Media Imperialism: towards an international framework for the analysis of media systems' in Curran, J. et al, *Mass Communication and Society*,

Edward Arnold, 1977.

Brunsdon, C., 'Feminism and Soap Opera' in Davies, K. et al, *Out of Focus – Writings on Women and the Media*, Women's Press, 1987.

Buckingham, D., *Public Secrets: Eastenders and its Audience*, British Film Institute, 1987.

Buckingham, D., 'Child's Play' in *The English and Media Magazine*, Summer 1994.

Burns, T., *The BBC: Public Institution and Private World*, Macmillan, 1977.

Cantril, H., *The Invasion from Mars: A Study in the Psychology of Panic*, Princeton University Press, 1940.

Cohen, S., *Folk Devils and Moral Panics*, Martin Robertson, 1980.

Collett, P., 'The Viewers Viewed' in *The Listener*, 22 May 1986.

Curran, J., Gurevitch, M. and Woollacott, J. (eds.), *Mass Communication and Society*, Edward Arnold, 1977.

Curran, J. and Seaton, J., *Power Without Responsibility*, Routledge, 1991.

Cumberbatch, G., *How the Miners Really Lost*, New Society, 23 May 1986.

Donnerstern, E., Linz, D. and Penrod, S., *The Question of Pornography*, Free Press, 1987.

Evans, H., *Good Times, Bad Times*, Weidenfeld and Nicholson, 1983.

Falcon, R., *Classified*, British Film Institute, 1994.

Franklin, B. and Murphy, D., *What's News? The Market, Politics and the Local Press*, Routledge, 1991.

Frazer, E., 'Teenage Girls Reading Jackie' in *Media Culture and Society*, 9 (4), 1987.

Gerbner, G. and Gross, L., 'Living with Television: The Violence Profile' in *Journal of Communication*, Vol. 28 No.3, 1976.

Gibson, P. and Gibson, R. (eds), *Dirty Looks: Women, Pornography power*, British Film Institute, 1993.

Gillespie, M., *Television, Ethnicity and Cultural Change*, Routledge, 1995.

Glasgow University Media Group, *More Bad News*, Routledge, 1980.

Glasgow University Media Group, *War and Peace News*, Open University Press, 1985.

Glinter, B., *Dimensions of Television Violence*, Gower, 1985.

Hazell, A. and Newburn, T., *Young Offenders and the Media*, PSI, 1994.

Hall, S. et al, *Policing the Crisis*, Macmillan, 1978.

Halloran, J. P., *The Effects of Television*, Panther, 1970.

Hartley, J., *Understanding News*, Methuen, 1982.

Hetherington, A., *News, Newspapers and Television*, Macmillan, 1985.

Hood, S., *On Television*, Pluto, 1980.

Inglis, F., *Media Theory*, Blackwell, 1990.

Katz, E. and Liebes, T., *The Export of Meaning*, Oxford University Press, 1990.

Kellner, D., *Media Culture*, Routledge, 1995.

Kutchinsky, B., 'Legalised Porn in Denmark' in Kimmel, M. (ed.), *Men Confront Pornography*, Crown, 1990.

Lezenfeld, P., Berelsen, B. and Gaudet, H., *The Peoples Choice*, Columbia University Press, 1968.

Leavis, F. R., *Mass Civilisation and Minority Culture*, Minority Press, 1930.

Lowery, A. and DeFleur, M., *Milestones in Mass Communication Research*, Longman, 1988.

Marcuse, H., *One Dimensional Man*, Routledge, 1964.

McDonald, M., *Representing Women*, Edward Arnold, 1995.

McLuhan, M., *Understanding Media*, Routledge, 1964.

McQuail, D. (ed.), *Sociology of Mass Communication*, Penguin, 1972.

McQuail, D., *Mass Communication Theory: an Introduction*, Sage, 1994.

McRobbie, A., 'The ideology of Jackie' in Waites, B., Bennett, T. and Martin, G., *Popular Culture: Past and Present*, Croom Helm, 1982.

Miller, W., *Media and Votes*, Clardendon Press, 1991.

Morley, D., *The 'Nationwide' Audience*, British Film Institute, 1980.

Mulvey, L., 'Visual Pleasure and narrative cinema' in *Screen*, 16 (3), 1975.

Murdock, G. and McCron, R., 'The Broadcasting and Delinquency Debate' in *Screen Education*, Spring, 1979.

Murdoch, G. and Golding, P. 'Capitalism, Communication and Class Relations' in Curran, J. et al, *Mass Communication and Society*, Edward Arnold, 1977.

Pearson, G., *Hooligan*, Macmillan, 1983.

Philo, G., *Seeing and Believing*, Routledge, 1990.

Powdermaker, H., *Hollywood, The Dream Factory*, Little Brown, 1950.

Reeves, G., *Communications and the 'Third World'*, Routledge. 1993.

Schlesinger, P. et al, *Women Viewing Violence*, British Film Institute, 199

Smith, A., *The Geopolitics of Information, How Western Culture Dominates the World*, Faber and Faber, 1980.

Storey, J., *An Introductory Guide to Cultural Theory and Popular Culture*, Harvester Wheatsheaf, 1993.

Strinati, D., *An Introduction to Theories of Popular Culture*, Routledge, 1995.

Thornton, S., *Club Cultures: Music Media and Subcultural Capital*, Polity, 1995.

Tuchman, G. et al. *Hearth and Home: Images of Women in Mass Media*, Free Press, 1978.

Williams, R., *Television, Technology and Cultural Form*, Routledge, 1990.

Further reading

The books listed below have been selected on the basis that they are reasonably accessible and they provide a more comprehensive coverage of the key issues introduced in this book.

Abercrombie, N. (1996) *Television and Society*, Polity.

Alvarado, M., Gutch, R., Wollen, T. (1987) *Learning the Media*, McMillan.

Baehr, H., Gray, A. (1996) *Turning it On – A Reader in Women and the Media*, Edward Arnold.

Branston, G., Stafford, R. (1996) *The Media Students Book*, Routledge.

Curran, J., Seaton, J. (1991) *Power Without Responsibility*, Routledge.

Ellis, J. (1992) *Visibile Fictions*, Routledge.

Goodwin, A., Whennel, G., eds. (1992) *Understanding Television*, Routledge.

Gray, A. (1992) *Video Playtime*, Routledge.

Gray, A., McGuigan, J. (1993) *Studying Culture – an introductory reader*, Edward Arnold.

Kellner, D. (1985) *Media Culture*, Routledge.

Lewis, P., Booth, J. (1989) *The Invisible Medium*, McMillan.

McDonald, M. (1995) *Representing Woman*, Edward Arnold.

McMahon, B., Quinn, R. (1986) *Real Images*, McMillan.

McNair, B. (1995) *An Introduction to Political Communication*, Routledge.

McNair, B. (1996) *News and Journalism in the UK*, Routledge.

Nelmes, J. (1996) *An Introduction to Film Studies*, Routledge.

O'Sullivan, T., Dutton, B., Rayner, P. (1994) *Studying the Media*, Edward Arnold.

Reeves, G. (1993) *Communications and the Third World*, Routledge.

Ross, K. (1996) *Black and White Media: Black Images in Popular Film and Television*, Polity.

Strineti, D. (1995) *An Introduction to Theories of Popular Culture*, Routledge.

Strineti, D., Wagg, S. (1992) *Come on Down: Popular Media Culture in Post War Britain*.

Tolson, A. (1996) *Mediation*, Edward Arnold.

Trowler, P. (1992) *Investigating the Media*, Collins.

Tunstall, J. (1996) *Newspaper Power: The New National Press in Britain*, Oxford University Press.

Index

Canal Street Gothic

David Thame

First published in England in 2011 by Pink Ewe Books
www.pinkewe.co.uk

These stories are fiction: it is all made up. Even so, Manchester
is not really so big, and gay Manchester is almost cosy.
With this in mind the writer begs the reader
to believe that any co-incidental similarities between characters in these
pages and living individuals are not because he's tried to smuggle
Manchester people into fiction, but thanks to the unusually
large number of fictional people who inhabit the real-life city.

Royalties from this edition have been assigned to
Albert Kennedy Trust (Registered charity number 1093815)
www.akt.org.uk

To V.B.T. who gave me stories, and to J.W. who gave me Manchester.

ISBN 978-0-9569354-0-3

Printed and bound by
Orphans Press Ltd, Leominster, Herefordshire HR6 0LD

Contents

Regulars

"So," says Paddy, who has been blowing kisses at bus drivers but now spins round to re-join the general conversation, "what's the theme?"

Gloomy Gary looks confused. "Do I need a theme?" he says.

"All parties need a theme," says Paddy.

It is about nine o'clock on a warm July evening and they are sitting, as they do every summer, at the last café table on Canal Street, the one closest to the New Union, the one next to Princess Street. They are not alone: along the full length of the street, spaced out among the recently planted trees next to the tow path wall are dozens of similar tables. Presided over by the New Union, for 150 years Canal Street has been Manchester's bohemian boulevard of love. Tonight, a Saturday, every table is occupied. Many new unions are in prospect.

"Your trouble," says Paddy, dragging a spare chair close and bracing his trainered feet against its seat, "your trouble is that you've no experience of this kind of thing." He takes a big gulp of his vodka and tonic, crunching the ice noisily between his teeth. "So the theme?" he says.

"Booze and sex," says Hugh, but his eyes are following someone in the crowd. It is the Sexy Northerner, who is now sauntering by their table listening intently to his companion, a tall blonde girl in white high heels. First Paddy and then Gary follow Hugh's glance and, in silence, they watch until the couple vanish from view, distant figures weaving through the street's many little knots of deoderised men in fresh t-shirts.

"Haven't seen her before," says Gary.

"Fag hag or girlfriend?" says Paddy.

Hugh makes a theatrical effort to catch a final glimpse of the couple. "I should say girlfriend," he says. "He likes a little walk in the lady garden, now and again."

"How do you know?" says Gloomy Gary.

"He made a confession," says Hugh, not meeting his Gary's eyes.

"Oh that time," says Paddy, beginning to play with the fringe on the table's pointless sunshade, "That time that didn't happen."

Hugh smiles. "We had a lovely evening, just the two of us up there," and he gestures vaguely towards Sackville Street, "on the roof pretending to watch for fire bombs. We talked about music and he explained how he did his hair. It looked so glossy in the light of the tracer flares."

"Did you get to take your bow-tie off?" asks Gloomy Gary.

"It was the war. We weren't in evening dress, dear," says Hugh.

"Never happier than in a uniform," says Gary. "Yes, you told us already."

Paddy stops fiddling with the fringe and stands up. "We need more drinks," he says. "My turn."

Hugh points at the table: his own white wine, Gary's lager, Paddy's vodka and tonic, each as full as the moment they were poured. "No need," he says. "We've plenty. We always have plenty," and fluttering his hand over the beverages he seems to bless them.

Once, perhaps, they sat somewhere else. Closer to the Rembrandt Hotel, for instance, or when it first opened years ago maybe they drank cold bottled beers on a table outside Taurus, daringly aware of the novelty of the drinks list and the danger of being so far down the wrong end of Canal Street. But it isn't certain. Nobody can remember, it has been so long. At some point this table near the New Union appeared, and they found themselves around it. None of them any longer thinks to complain. Hugh, with his sleek hair and his wide high-waisted trousers, Paddy in his street gear, Gloomy Gary in the same white shirt and drip-dry trousers he was wearing when, in 1991, the police pulled him from his fume-filled car; if anyone had seen them they would have appeared an unlikely mix. But no one ever seems to see them.

Tonight the street is in merrymaking mood. Until late yesterday it had been raining, raining for days as only Manchester rain can, insidiously creeping inside coats and under doors and falling not straight down, like normal rain, but soaking and seeping in any direction. For days the street has been deserted. But in the small hours the clouds cleared and the sky dried up. Tonight, then, everyone who can get to the street is here, or will be soon, because this is the kind of meteorological chance you would not want to miss.

"There's Bev," says Paddy, waving extravagantly at a ginger-haired girl in black. "Bev, over here." The girl smiles and detaches herself from a festive-sized woman in sandals and loose white cotton pyjamas.

"Do you have to?" says Gary as the girl approaches. Paddy ignores him.

"So you're all here," she says in a strong town accent, kissing Paddy on both cheeks.

"Where else?" says Hugh. "We're always here."

Bev settles herself in the fourth chair.

"Who is she, then?" says Paddy pointing at the pyjamas, "The new squeeze?"

"Wendy," says Bev. "But she goes by the professional name of Avalon. She talks to people on the other side."

Paddy gives her an appraising look.

"Did you see....?" he asks.

"Yes, I did see," says Bev, "with a girl on his arm. We," and she gestures towards Avalon, who is now flourishing two green glass beer bottles at her in a jovial manner, "we think it's his sister."

"No!" says Paddy.

"She's come over from Leeds," says Bev. "Or so Avalon says."

Hugh studies Avalon over his glass.

"The white high heels....?" suggests Paddy.

Bev stands up. "I know," she says and she skips back towards her lover like a schoolgirl.

"Sister be damned," says Hugh.

"Perhaps I'll ask him to my party," says Gloomy Gary. "Then we'll see."

"You're not in his league, darling," says Hugh.

Gloomy Gary drains his plastic glass. He says: "Everybody who lives on this planet knows that good looks and sexual magnetism have nothing to do with one another."

"And what if you don't live on this planet?" says Paddy.

"Precisely," says Hugh.

■

The street is now crowded: outside the New Union the thirty-something men who spent the early evening talking quietly or sharing a bottle of wine are being replaced under the sunshades by rowdy fives or sixes, giggling pre-party boy groups that have to borrow chairs from other tables, or sit on each other's laps. Outside Manto the teenage crowd is milling and swirling, sometimes eddying out to include attractive examples of the slightly older Gap-clads leaning against the towpath wall. Through the middle of all this, turning the corner from Richmond Street and into Canal Street proper, comes a procession. At the front is a man in snorkel mask and grass skirt, swaying and half-dancing to the Mama Cass song blasting full volume from the ghetto blaster he is carrying. Behind him are half a dozen waggling weasel-faced young men in board shorts, dark glasses and flip flops, each holding a flaming torch and handing out promotional leaflets: Tonight @ Triple X,

A Beach Party! More or less maintaining their formation they noisily progress through the throng, a giggling amateurish affront to health and safety.

The procession passes just inches from their table, so close indeed that the table might have been invisible. A leaflet flutters to the floor by Hugh's spit-and-polished shoes. Picking it up Paddy says: "Shall we?"

"It would be too loud for me," says Hugh, scanning the crowd as if looking for someone. "I'm more of a big band man. But go if you want to."

"You can't go. None of you can. What about my party?" says Gary.

"Of course," says Paddy. "Your party. Mustn't forget that." He swirls the few remaining chips of ice around his vodka and tonic and drains it in one mouthful. "Think I'll just go and have a look around. You know, do a bit of shopping."

Hugh pulls a face. "Don't you mean selling?" he says.

"Old habits," says Paddy, flipping his hood over his head so that his small sharp face is shaded and hidden.

"I'll stop here," says Gloomy Gary, answering a question nobody asked. "What would be the point?" Paddy puts his empty glass back on the table, gives the sunshade a farewell spin, and is soon lost in the crowd.

Gloomy Gary coughs and a little petrol-blue cloud of toxins and carbon monoxide floats out of his mouth and up into the canopy of the sunshade where it dissolves languidly.

Watching the last wisp vanish Hugh says: "You don't have to stay with me."

For a few moments they study the crowd. Soon a familiar figure emerges as if their need had called him into existence. The figure heads purposefully for the tow path wall.

"Now look at that," says Hugh. Gloomy Gary follows his glance.

The Sexy Northerner is leaning against the wall just a few yards from their table, his foot braced against it. He is casually running a hand through his perfect hair. He looks at the late evening crowd and spotting Hugh mouths "Hi." Hugh smiles and raises his glass in salute.

"See," Hugh says to Gary. "We go way back."

"Back to the night the warehouse on Sackville Street was blown sky high?" says Gary.

"You needn't adopt that weary tone," says Hugh, still waving and smiling. "All the boys used to go there. It was a very sociable place during the blackout. Especially just before Christmas."

Gary describes rapid circular wind-it-up movements with his left hand. Hugh raises his eyebrows and reaches for his glass. "I was just buttoning up my flies when I thought 'that one sounds like it's going to be rather close.' It was a direct hit."

Gary yawns affectedly. "Paddy tells a different story," he says, nodding towards the Sexy Northerner. "Says he worked with him out of the bus station café. Would pretend to need a quid for the coach, on the corner of Minshull Street. His speciality was one minute blow jobs on the NCP staircase."

Hugh sips thoughtfully then shakes his head. "How would he know? Trust me," he says, "in Paddy's line of work you don't look at people's faces."

They drink in silence and watch as the Sexy Northerner is joined by a lithe-looking man in his early twenties carrying a bottle of champagne. There is the usual performance as he pulls off the foil and the cork pops like a rifle shot. None of the men near them seems to notice. He pours, they drink, they kiss, they laugh.

"A chorus boy," says Hugh. "You can tell from his legs."

"I wish someone would buy me a bottle of champagne," says Gary. "Nobody ever did."

"Count your blessings," says Hugh, and indicates the table in front of them where the three glasses are once again full. "So how did you...?" he asks.

"God knows. Probably from the cottage on Oxford Road. It could have been anyone," says Gary, "I expect I've still got the clinic's appointment card here," and he pats the front pocket of his shirt where Hugh can indeed see through the drip-dry cotton a small rectangle of discoloration. For a moment this image is familiar — have they had this conversation before? Hugh cannot remember.

Paddy suddenly drops back into his seat. "Whoa," he says, pretending to wipe the sweat from his brow. He takes his glass and gulps dramatically. "I needed that."

"Been flinging yourself about?" says Gary. Paddy nods as if, in his condition, words are impossible.

"Guess who's back in town," says Hugh, nodding significantly at the Sexy Northerner.

Paddy waves and calls to the two men who break their embrace, the dancer to wave back and the Sexy Northerner to give a thumbs up.

"So, this party," says Paddy, folding his arms as if braced for hard decisions. "Who's coming?"

■

There has been a change of mood in the street, a change that owes as much to mathematics as to hormones. The crowd is now dense like a popular nightclub: newcomers must edge sideways, pressing their way to pre-arranged dates or to surprising new ones. But their advance is slow and halting, delayed as drinks are ferried at head-height from the bars, or as little conversational groups form and reform. Some are suddenly expelled from the mass into a gap miraculously (and briefly) empty, or escape by spotting and then claiming a vacant space between the men leaning on the tow path wall. Here, if they haven't yet lost their friends in the crush, they will lean over the stone parapet and tell each other the story of how last summer the body of a rent boy, named in the papers as Patrick James Molloy, was found face down in the hardly-moving water. And so, at this time in the evening, Canal Street is all about calculations: how long will it take to get served at the bar, what is my chance of spotting him or him spotting me, how likely is it that I, too, will go home with the wrong guy and end up in the canal with the pizza boxes and the Coke cans? Decimals and fractions, all converted into futures.

Paddy has fallen silent and is himself looking into the dark canal.

13

"In my day," Hugh is beginning.

"Oh spare us," says Gloomy Gary, "your tales of air-raids and blackouts and the ever-friendly black GI Joes in the New Union. We've heard it all a thousand times before."

"You weren't there," says Hugh.

"For heaven's sake," says Paddy. "Just for one night, ok?"

Gary reaches for his lager and notices that the Sexy Northerner is no longer folded around the dancer but is now pressed close to someone else, someone female amply filling a pair of loose white cotton pyjamas. They are holding hands, fingers intertwined, and she is looking into his eyes but he is not returning the gaze. Instead he looks discretely over her shoulder, almost as if he were a policeman on surveillance duty, and as she pushes closer, apparently pressing her knee into his groin, he turns to Gary and, with cool deliberation, winks at him.

Hugh is now standing next to Paddy who is leaning on the stone parapet watching the reflections of the bar lights in the cold black water, water in which not long ago he was found arms out and face down.

"Not the Styx, more's the pity," says Hugh to Paddy.

Paddy doesn't reply. He is staring in the direction of a little polystyrene curry-sauce pot which seems to be floating towards lock gates and eventually towards the tunnel under Piccadilly, the tunnel where once upon a time he was so busy and so popular.

"So my party, then. Is it time?" says Gary.

"Definitely," says Hugh, taking his seat again. "We all need a bit of cheering up."

"You too, Paddy?" asks Gary. Paddy gives the sunshade a vigorous slap and for a few seconds it spins merrily, its fringe flapping and batting like eyelashes. "Spose so," he says. "We can go to my apartment."

"Your apartment?" says Hugh.

"Perhaps not quite mine," says Paddy. "You know how it is."

Gloomy Gary stands up and, drinking his plastic glass dry, flings the tumbler into the canal. They all watch its twisting flight and its landing so gentle that there is barely a ripple. "Come along," he says. "That's enough for tonight."

Paddy finishes his drink too.

"Don't worry about booze," says Hugh. "There's always booze."

They push their chairs back and move out into the human flood, walking together silently and unseen down busy Canal Street, and as they do so they are joined by the Sexy Northerner and Avalon, by Bev and the dancer and the girl in white high heels, and by dozens of other regulars who you will not have seen sitting in twos and threes at other invisible tables, souls of the party every one. The transparent procession walks through a door that is not there, up stairs that do not exist, to a flat in a building on Sackville Street that was blown up long ago.

Cock-Lorel:
An Unmade Film, circa 1989

1. EXT. A BACK ALLEY IN CENTRAL MANCHESTER. DAY.

Now here he is, LOREL, young Lorel, loitering in the dark and dirty obscurity of Manchester's Back Piccadilly. He has just the right clothes, just the right haircut, and skin that is almost criminally pale. He is Lorel the dandy, Lorel the madman, the youth with the dangerous eyes.

2. EXT. MARKET STREET. MANCHESTER. DAY

Only yards away, on the other side of soot-blackened buildings and rusting fire escapes, the Saturday morning shoppers are going about their business.

3. EXT. THE BACK ALLEY. DAY.

Lighting a cigarette, LOREL, cock of the walk, a king among men, also goes about his business. Shimmering and insinuating himself out of Back Piccadilly into Spear Street and from there into Dale Street, he moves smoothly and sexually as if he were in nightclub.

4. EXT. OLDHAM STREET. DAY

A wide shot of a busy street corner.

The pedestrian flow is stronger in Dale Street: untidy scavengers, youths of all kinds, old people, Elizabethan driftwood. Well trusty LOREL stands on the corner by the record store, looking down Oldham Street towards the city's more prosperous shops, taking a drag on his cigarette, then glancing the other way up to New Cross and the badlands of Ancoats.

5. EXT. OLDHAM STREET. DAY

Close up on LOREL's face: his glance lingers on New Cross. Maybe he's seen something, or someone? Then a wider shot: he looks back over his shoulder, drops the cigarette, and screws the butt into the pavement with the heel of his trainers. And he does this all in one movement, fluidly, like an actor. Then he's off, turns the corner down Oldham Street, his patch, his special place, a jaunty easy possessive walk just forty yards towards the newsagents.

6. INT. NEWSAGENTS. DAY.

LOREL knows the shop well, another of his haunts, a place out of the rain to browse and plan. A few pleasantries with the TILL GIRL are not out of place. LOREL picks up a copy of the Manchester Evening News.

LOREL: And a packet of Rislas. Brown. (He pauses) You alright?

TILL GIRL (not meeting his glance): Great.

She hands him his change and the Rislas. Neither of them smile.

Green-eyed LOREL pockets his money and clocks the other customers: from LOREL's P.O.V. we see an old woman reading a magazine, a younger man in a suit reaching up to the top shelf. Nothing to LOREL's taste, perhaps? LOREL leaves and the P.O.V.

remains in the shop, roughly where the TILL GIRL has been standing, so that LOREL is seen walking briskly, almost swaggering, through the door and then glimpsed through the shop window which is covered in posters and stranded spots of blu-tak.

7.   EXT. OLDHAM STREET. DAY.

LOREL stands and opens his newspaper. He is on the corner outside the Merchants Hotel, at the junction of Back Piccadilly and Oldham Street, and about twenty yards from where he began. Another circuit completed, the third or fourth by this time of day, about noon on a promising Saturday morning.

8.   EXT. OLDHAM STREET. DAY.

Standing by the hotel door LOREL is reading his newspaper. Around him shops and shoppers of various kinds — fashionable, low, illegal. The sky is heavy, cloudy and threatening; it's humid, there might be thunder. We see from LOREL's P.O.V. that directly opposite him are the Famous Army Stores, and next to it the entrance to the first-floor gymnasium. Traffic passes. LOREL knows in alchemical ways that this is a place where baseness turns golden. Among the litter and gritty bus fumes of Oldham Street, his home, his very own, LOREL shifts his weight from one foot to the other with his infallible sense of style.

9.   EXT. OLDHAM STREET. DAY

LOREL is not long waiting, if waiting is what he's been doing. Close-up of LOREL's face — he thinks he's sighted someone coming out of the Famous Army Stores. Then from LOREL'S P.O.V. we see THE FRIEND: young, fashionably dressed, clean shaven, he's the obvious magnet for a character like LOREL who, with no sign of hurry, folds his newspaper and puts it in the back pocket of his jeans. Scarcely looking at the traffic he crosses the busy road.

10. INT. NEWSAGENTS. DAY

The P.O.V. is again inside the newsagents, through the window. We see LOREL trot lightly across the road, not quite running, not quite a walk, weaving between the buses. He stops THE FRIEND. We see LOREL speak, gesticulate — maybe he points down Oldham Street, then LOREL puts his hands deep in his pockets. LOREL is an adept at this game, he knows every move and counter-move; he is a grand master of street encounters. The opening gambit hardly matters — he just has to say something and then keep talking. Invariably LOREL talks about his clothes.

11. EXT. OLDHAM STREET. DAY

P.O.V. from the top of a building, looking down: snatches of LOREL's conversation are briefly and distantly heard over the bus engines.

LOREL: I don't like to look like a slob or a tramp, because I'm not a tramp. See this jacket? D'you know how much this jacket cost? More than you earn in a month.

The rest of their conversation is lost in the traffic.

LOREL has one sure and certain rule, his unique selling point: never accept money. He'll turn it down, look offended, maybe even threaten you (did you know he carries a knife?). Whatever else he is — and if you're the right person he'll risk a smile about now — he's not like that. You've got him wrong, thanks but no thanks.

So LOREL the roaring boy, Lorel the leader of men, becomes as he talks Lorel the lonely, Lorel your best mate, a pal, and since you've been talking and getting on so well, why not come and have a coffee? Just a coffee. He only lives up the road. Fifteen minutes of your time, that's all. Its great (and here he might smile again) to have someone intelligent to talk to.

It never fails.

12.   EXT. BUSY CROSSROADS. DAY

Another wide shot: Manchester looks more than ever like the Lower East Side of New York: big buildings, wide streets, danger, dirt. P.O.V. still from the top of a building, following LOREL and the FRIEND. From the junction of Back Piccadilly with Oldham Street they walk east towards Church Street. At the cross-roads they turn left into Church Street. They pass Afflecks Palace, the car park, the market stalls, the kerbs stacked with boxes of rotting fruit and the gutters choked with cabbage leaves. They turn right into long, narrow and pavement-less Tib Street — and out of our vision.

13.   EXT. DARK NARROW ALLEY. DAY

Tib Street reeks of Tudor squalor. LOREL knows it well, knows every one of its newsagents and sex shops, its ill-lit pet shops, and the doors at street level that never close, doors that lead up dirty staircases to paradise or purgatory. It is through one of these never-closing doors that LOREL the rogue, the great pretender, leads his new FRIEND. By now heavy thunder clouds have gathered. The daylight is weak — it is just after 1pm but might be late evening. As the two men ascend the stairs a police car with its headlights on drives slowly and deliberatively along the road.

14.   INT. STAIRCASE. DAY.

We see them from the front, in silhouette, coming up the stairs then turning into an open door lit from within by faint rainy daylight. THE FRIEND is the first up the stairs and he pauses before the door. LOREL taps him on the shoulder, and indicates another door — closed — on the far side of the small landing.

15.   INT. LOREL'S ROOM. DAY.

The room is dirty and largely empty; there is a stained, damp-looking, single mattress on the floor; a chair; pages from a newspaper are scattered around. As LOREL and THE FRIEND enter there is the sound of sudden heavy rain driving against the window. THE FRIEND looks around.

LOREL (as he leaves the room): Coffee?

FRIEND: Yes. Thanks.

16.   EXT. TIB STREET OUTSIDE THE ROOM. DAY.

The police car, still with its headlights on, has stopped. A policewoman with a clipboard gets out of the car and knocks on one of the closed — apparently derelict — doors. She waits a few seconds, then scuttles back into the car, using the clipboard to protect herself from the downpour.

17.   INT. LOREL'S ROOM. DAY.

Close up, from the inside, of the rain thundering onto the window, then panning round we see LOREL and the FRIEND standing, kissing passionately.

18.   INT. STAIRCASE. EVENING.

Viewed from the top of the staircase, looking down to the open street door. Someone rounds the corner into view, then hurries down the stairs. It is LOREL but we see only his silhouette against the light from outside, taking two steps at a time, then leaping the last few, then out into the puddled street.

19. INT. LOREL'S ROOM. EVENING.

Gentle rain on the window, then we pan to an empty packet of cigarettes, recently crunched up in someone's fist, discarded on the mattress. A hand moves into our view, and flicks the packet onto the floor. The shot widens to show the hand belongs to THE FRIEND, propped up on his other arm. He is laying on and amongst his clothes. The magic that has ravished him is broken.

20. EXT. OLDHAM STREET. NIGHT.

Leaning on a lamp post, once again back on his beat at the corner of Oldham Street and Back Piccadilly, LOREL lights a cigarette. Close up on his face as he takes a puff. He is beautiful. In five minutes he will make another circuit. Oldham Street is still busy — young people and rough people mixing on the dirty pavement. Some are getting off fully-lit but almost empty buses. The metal shutters are down outside the Famous Army Stores. The door to the gymnasium is locked.

LOREL drops the cigarette: the focus remains on his face but it is clear from his body movements that he is screwing it into pavement with his shoe. Instead of turning into Back Piccadilly he walks along Oldham Street and towards the traffic lights. He reaches the junction with Market Street and from his P.O.V. we see that it is now virtually free of pedestrians — just a few giggling girls walking arm in arm past brightly lit but empty shops. It is very late.

LOREL looks up. Extreme close-up on his eyes — we see reflections of coloured neon. Then cut to LOREL'S P.O.V to see, burning on the topless tower of Piccadilly Plaza huge illuminated advertisements for personal computers, drinks, photographic film.

21. EXT. PICCADILLY PLAZA. NIGHT

Cut to the the view from the top of Piccadilly Plaza: we see LOREL distant and small on the far side of the largely empty square among the buses and taxis in the sodium orange street-light. Usual late Saturday evening scene. For a moment LOREL appears to meet our gaze, but surely he cannot see us, we are too far away? He turns and walks — the credits roll — and when he is finally out of vision, fade to black.

A Deansgate Afternoon

"Really?" Denis is saying into the telephone, "Really? Silly cow. What's she frightened of? Well can you try again? Please? Thanks."

You know what this office looks like: you have seen it a thousand times before. An overlit prairie of desks and computer screens, water coolers by pillars, photocopiers in corners, low waist-height partitioning separating one team from another. It's very ordinary, completely the way you'd expect it to be, this bright new newspaper office off Manchester's Deansgate.

The phone rings.

"Business desk. Yes. Yes. About half an hour. Yes. Bye." Denis puts the receiver down and studies the piece of paper in front of him. It is from a department that used to be called personnel but is now called something more coldly manipulative. He decides to read it later — besides, he knows what it says without reading it, has known in fact since the envelope arrived with the internal post about ten o'clock this morning.

The phone rings again.

"Business desk. Dave, thanks for calling back. I've got your copy in front of me. No, nothing serious. Para two, line two, it says Sainsburys. Do you mean J Sainsbury? Or is there another firm called Sainsburys because if there is I don't know what it is. You meant J Sainsbury? Yes, just checking. Thanks. Thank you."

That was cruel, of course it was. But sometimes you have to be cruel to be kind. Or to be cruel. Or simply to be. Anyway, two-thirty. Two hours to go.

This isn't the kind of office where there's anything to be gained from a seat by the window: although the Manchester traffic is only a few dozen yards away the view is of other office blocks which look as blank as this one. That's why Denis isn't bothered about the whereabouts of his workstation. Although he was bothered once. Too close to the sports desk he used to think, but now he's not so sure.

He studies the screen: simple errors, but everyone makes them. Take the first sentence, reverse it, place the subject before the object, and straight away it reads better. Delete that quote further down, cut the next paragraph in half — it's repetitious. Headline? Tight little space, it would have to be two words, five letters and three letters, or five and four. Deals Joy. Done Deals. Big Deals. D-day Deals. Deals D-day.

Where are the pictures for the retail story? Nothing in his inbox, no attachments with the copy. Another call to be made. And of course there was still that stupid bitch who didn't want her picture taken. Did she really think they were going to use a holiday snap? Some people.

There was an explosion of laughter on the other side of the partition.

"Andy, could you please keep the noise down?" Denis shouts.

"Sorry Den, got carried away."

"No problem, its just a bit..."

"Yes, sorry."

Nice guy, but he never stops: cars, football, cars, football. Proper little lad. Writing not too bad — a few clichés and loaded with over-achieving adjectives, but that's what sports reporting is all about. Making very little go a very long way.

'Deals D-day' it would have to be. Denis begins to type but the computer screen slides away from him, the characters tumbling into chaos in the right hand corner. For a moment he's confused, his fingers won't find the keyboard. But even as it is happening he knows what it means, and knows that it will pass. Slowly the screen re-assembles itself. He types: d-e-a-l-s-D-day. It's ok. Everything's ok.

The phone rings.

"Business desk. I see. Yes. Have you tried telling her that we can't run the story of her bloody stupid life and her bloody stupid company and her bloody stupid job without a bloody picture? Ok. Well, do your best. Bye."

The computer screen is once again stable and usable. He clicks on another file. A new supermarket is to be opened.... Scratch that. High Street giant J Sainsbury is to.... Delete 'high street.' Supermarket giant J Sainsbury.... Much better. Jobs? Is there a number for new jobs? There is — pull that up to the top, the punters like that sort of thing. The move will create 70 new jobs, say bosses. Says the firm. Say Sainsbury bosses.

He picks up the receiver and taps a 3-digit internal number. The call is answered immediately.

"It's me. Fine, thanks. Look, we've got a problem with the profile. Yes. Yes. She shouldn't have agreed in the first place, it was all explained. Have you..... Right. Yes. Well that would do, I suppose. Yes, please. Bye."

Andy is over at the water-cooler with the trainee from features. Are they talking about him? It is possible. It is very likely. They were looking his way and would be saying "The business desk has been useless since Bill left. Den just can't cope." And both young enough to be his son. His sons. Each was young enough to be his son.

The clock on the wall says five to three.

Denis is now moving papers around his desk, tearing some things up, putting others into files, or the bin or into the drawer. His desk is always tidy — everyone says "Do you want to do my desk next?" or "I bet you roll your socks into pairs," or they say something else, often pointing the contrast with the disorder of Bill's desk when he was in charge, because the tidiness of Den's never goes unremarked. The letter that he still hasn't read is tidy, too: it has been folded and put into the pocket of the grey suit jacket which is hanging over the back of his chair.

Editorial conference at half past. He should go. He should go but will not go. The profile fiasco is unresolved, and the rest of the copy is subbed, in the system and ready to roll, so there is nothing he could say.

Phone again, flashing an internal call.

"Yes? I'm doing my best but the bitch.... Yes. Yes. I'm too busy. Yes." Receiver smashed down.

They didn't really expect him at the conference anyway: nobody would expect him. Now, knowing he wouldn't walk in, they could talk about him in safety. Silly bloody queen: they could say that if he stayed away. Denis rubs his forehead. Where has this migraine come from so suddenly?

Perhaps if he called someone? (This bloody head) Perhaps he should. He was sure he should. Denis was sure he should call someone. And if he did, what would they say? Only what he knew anyway: about last time and what happened and (this bloody headache). They probably didn't even know he had friends, or a family, or a lover — didn't think it possible that he had a life at all, away from this desk and from Deansgate. Personnel would know, of course. Next of kin was on file.

Denis reaches for the telephone, but the merest movement makes the space between his left ear and his left eye throb with such a fierce intensity that his arm drops back onto the desk. He says to himself: this bloody bloody head be calm be calm count backwards from ten nine eight seven six five four three two one big deep breath.

The pain begins to ease: through half open eyes he scans the desk in front of him.

Telephone, stapler, two pens, a yellow note stuck to the computer screen, and the latest production schedule pinned to the low partition walling. No framed photographs, no pictures cut from magazines, no mottoes, no mascots. He raises his head, straightens himself in his chair, and clicks open another file.

"Coming to the conference, Den?" It is Andy, leaning over the partition, notepad ready. Denis keeps his eyes on the screen and continues typing. "I've got to finish this. There's nothing I can tell them," Denis says.

"Ok," says Andy then, pausing: "Sure everything's all right? You look whacked."

"For crying out loud..." Denis complains, but Andy is saying "ok, ok" and walking away before the sentence gets any further.

Denis watches Andy follow the others into the meeting room. They would talk about that too now, about how Denis was loosing it, how it was no surprise, not really. "Not a team player..." which of course Bill had been, with his evenings in the Sawyers Arms, his long lunches, his banter and shoulder-punching and back-slapping. Not a team player meaning not on our team, the men's team, the lad's team. Not one of us. The telephone rings — internal call again.

"Any progress? You did — good. Why? No, I don't believe it. No. After two flaming fucking wasted days. How on earth does she imagine we can get a photographer there in time? I'll have to think. Yes, of course. I'll call you back."

There is one hour to go.

Denis is scrolling through his email inbox: he's looking for stories that could fill the gap left by the soon-to-be-spiked profile. He has identified several press releases that might do — would have to do, given the circumstances. A few of them already come pre-packaged with pictures. He picks up the phone and jabs at the keypad. It rings. He waits. Then: "Look, forget it. Forget her — she's had her chance. We'll just have to scrub it. Pull the lot. Yes, no choice. I'll see what we can throw together. No, I'll find something. Ok. Thanks."

Denis can see them all in the meeting room: someone is speaking, others are watching, writing or looking into the middle distance. No one is smiling. What could they be saying? He'd discover, of course, even if it was an edited version. It would be written all over their faces.

He selects one of the promising email messages, opens its attachment and whilst he is correcting and shaping the text on the computer screen — making sure that a company is singular not plural, checking that the past tense is used for news stories and the present tense for features — in his head he is correcting the letter in his grey jacket pocket. 'We are sorry that, on this occasion, we must decline...': strike 'on this occasion' — otiose, redundant, sounds like a policeman reading his evidence in court. Delete 'we' and say I: too pompous. For 'decline' substitute 'refuse' — because you cannot decline an application. You refuse applications, you decline invitations, but the silly girl in human so-called resources has probably never ... . Suddenly he cannot look at the screen. The headache has returned and is violently stabbing at the back of his left eye. Heavy knives seem to be moving smoothly back and forward inside his brain, cutting and re-cutting, their weight taking them deeper with each stoke. As the pain grows Denis shuts his eyes and holds the desk and for a moment, a short but very alarming moment, he feels a tingling tightness on the left side of his head as if the skin round his skull is suddenly gripping him. Then he is tumbling and falling fast, spiralling down and over, but he hangs onto the desk and the vertigo ebbs away from him slowly, like a wave withdrawing.

He opens his eyes, blinking, to discover that everything looks wrong, is both too close and too far away at the same time. The computer, and behind it the schedules pinned to the partition, seem flattened, without depth or perspective. The screen in particular is unreadable. His head still screaming Denis reaches down into the draw for one of the special screen wipes he likes to use and it is only as he begins to clean the monitor that he realises his left eye is not working.

There are five minutes to go.

The editorial conference is ending, or has ended: colleagues are spilling out of the meeting room in ones and twos, some of them talking and apparently amused, others heading back to their desks. Denis knows why they are laughing. The chaos of the missing profile will have given them the excuse they needed. Denis watches them disperse, heads and shoulders threading through the workstations and partitions, before dropping out of sight and onto their chairs each vanishing in turn like rabbits leaping down holes. The calm surface of office life is restored.

Denis knows that now it is his turn to stand up. He tells himself that he will walk calmly and conspicuously to the editor's office, he will mention the letter he received this morning, and he will ask why he has not been chosen. Hasn't he kept the show on the road since Bill left? Hasn't he shown himself capable of running the business desk, despite being short staffed, despite everything? Hasn't he years of loyal service behind him and many more years of conscientious effort ahead? He reaches round to hook his grey jacket off the chair. His arm from the shoulder down feels numb and unusually weak. He pushes his chair back and braces himself to stand,

and as he does so the right hand side of his body seems to melt onto the floor.

"It looks like he's choking. We should move him into the recovery position," someone is saying and another voice, different from the first, says: "You ok Den?" but Denis does not understand: he can hear sounds, but not words. He can see his chair on its side next to him, and he can see a hand that might be his own very close to his face, but he cannot work out how his body is arranged or how the hand got there. He cannot feel the hand. It isn't his. His tongue is not there or will not move. He cannot swallow.

"You OK, Den?" someone asks again, but it has no meaning. Deletions and substitutions are being reversed, emendations erased, sentences returning to the chaos in which he found them. The mind that was once a carefully marked page is becoming a mass of unstructured scribble.

Dr Nizami's Pizzas

Have you ever eaten in Casa Bolognese? Probably. Almost everyone has, or somewhere like it. The walls are artfully crusted with rough grotto-style plaster and the ceiling is as low as the light. In one corner there is a small unfashionable-looking bar lined with half-empty bottles of Strega and Limoncello. There are red paper napkins on the tables and, by the kitchen door, there is a tank of tropical fish. The menu, which is large and laminated, promises penne picante and quatro formaggio and the drinks list includes Fanta, sold by the can. Casa Bolognese is small and popular and has been feeding the students of Fallowfield for twenty years. It is a success and so, it follows logically, is Dr Nizami.

Antipasti

If you are planning to emigrate to Manchester it is best to do so when the economy is booming, and not when it is bust. Dr Nizami got this wrong. When he arrived in 1990 Manchester was bust. Deansgate, which he believed to be the Bond Street of the North, was half derelict; the Free Trade Hall, possessor of a magical name he associated with British liberty and World Service broadcasts, was a chilly hulk; Piccadilly was dangerous and Oldham Street much worse. In all, Dr Nizami told himself, the place barely looked like England.

He might have been disappointed but in fact he wasn't. Somehow the dampness and darkness seemed to multiply the actual physical miles he had travelled into many more psychological miles, and this made him feel safe and happy. Whatever this place was, it wasn't Kuwait. That was what mattered.

The Manchester Dr Nizami moved to — the wrecked glory that existed before trams and smart hotels and city-living apartments — was now his now home and he set out to explore it. A fearless pedestrian, he bought a cheap plastic anorak from the underground market and slowly, A to Z in hand, assembled a list of personal landmarks. He discovered the Holman Hunts in the deserted art gallery and he sat in the great round reading room of the Central Library where he read with anxiety the day-before-yesterday's Arab language newspapers. Dr Nizami thought he was in paradise. Every gutter-brown puddle or unsmiling shop assistant delighted him because they proved, simply and directly, how very far he was from the Persian Gulf. He wrote long ecstatic letters saying this to his brother and to Mrs Nizami, his wife

Not that Manchester was without its perplexities. Finding a room to rent was easy, but the rooms he was shown were neither clean nor nice. This was dispiriting. There was prejudice too, and this was worse because it was surprising. Dr Nizami had not expected crude prejudice in an imperial power — after all, the Ottomans had managed to avoid it — and he reasoned that in a trading city like Manchester it was surely self-defeating? But there it was — brutal and unavoidable — a fact of his new life. Confronted, then, with a choice between being a wop or a paki — and being a Kuwaiti-Azerbaijani he was neither — in 1990 Dr Nizami chose to be a wop. To his amazement he passed for an Italian without any further question and, cautiously at first but then with confidence, he substituted for the heavy handsomeness of his real first name, Suhail, the light and unfamiliar sportiness of Gino.

And then he had his idea, the idea that changed everything. Living in a shared house in Fallowfield, with only the mould in the bathroom for company and a great deal of time to himself, Dr Nizami fell into the habit of eating out. It wasn't long before he realised that the real arena of opportunity was not in building bridges (the subject of his thesis in civil engineering) but in that of cheap and decent student food served in a vaguely Mediterranean ambiance. He made plans, saved and borrowed, gradually became genial Gino, and the Casa Bolognese — Casa Bollocks to many generations of students — opened in time for summer term 1991. It hasn't had a quiet night since.

Primo Piatto

Those first few months of 1991 saw several great improvements in Dr Nizami's quality of life. In early February he hired a car, filled the boot with his precious Arabic books, covered the back seat with clothes and drove the quarter mile from his unhappy little rented room to the much larger flat which filled the two floors above what would soon be Casa Bolognese. It was his own private space, large, airy, sanitary and, above all, dry. This last point mattered enormously: it had been a particularly cold and wet winter and Dr Nizami had often seriously wondered, as he watched the pages of paperbacks curl and his spare overcoat develop a grey bloom, whether anything he possessed would ever be genuinely damp-free again. In time he would come to regard this all-embracing atmospheric wetness as a normal feature of Manchester life, and would, like all Mancunians challenged by outsiders, angrily deny any abnormal humidity or rainfall. But not that first winter. Definitely not.

The second big augmentation of comfort was Dr Nizami's discovery that he was not alone in Manchester. It wasn't that Dr. Nizami didn't already have friends — quite the contrary — but rather that the people he met were unsatisfactory. You see, his first contacts in Manchester had been had been in the shifting world of landlords and fellow lodgers. Some had been enjoyable companions and others interesting case studies, but none were of any duration: relationships were soon begun, soon matured, and soon over. One day they were solid people one met on the stairs or outside bathrooms, the next they were mere names on unopened envelopes piled up by the front door. Inevitably Dr Nizami found this unfulfilling.

In the world beyond the bedsit Dr Nizami mixed with the city's Armenians and Kurds, spending many sociable evenings and smiling afternoons with them in distant suburbs and unfamiliar districts. They were numerous, but reminded him too much of home. He let these contacts drop. No, the people Dr Nizami really discovered, the people he cared about, were his staff at Casa Bolognese.

Terry was the third potential cook Dr Nizami interviewed. He was short, had City Forever tattooed on his arm, a flat bridge to his nose, and generally looked like a boxer which, in fact, is what he had been during his time in the army catering corps. They first met one afternoon in the half-refurbished restaurant. Surrounded by builders' rubble and chaos Dr Nazimi leaned on what would become the bar and Terry stood in the spot where the fish tank would one day go. Dr Nazimi explained that they would serve cheap, decent, filling food, to students who would come back week after week. Terry said ace and triffic, and made some very sensible suggestions about ice-cream and within a few minutes it seemed the most natural thing in the world to offer him the job. Later, with Terry to advise, a cheap fitted kitchen was installed. With days to go before the first service Terry worked on his costings and made long loud telephone calls to wholesalers. Dr. Nizami was full of frank admiration. After a few hesitations and false starts — moussaka was in, then it was out — the restaurant menu solidified into the successful form it has to this day.

Soon the team had grown to four: a nice girl with dreadlocks called Avril was to be the waitress, and on Terry's recommendation Dr Nizami recruited Gaz, a dangerous-looking lad from Northenden whose older brother used to train in Terry's gym. Gaz became the kitchen porter. Together they delivered leaflets to every student house in Fallowfield and every student hall of residence in Owens Park.

It was raining heavily the evening Casa Bolognese opened. By the time the first customers arrived Dr Nizami had almost given up hope. It might have been a slow start, but Casa Bolognese was soon busy. When Dr Nizami realised that customers were still arriving even though it was well after 11pm he decided to stay open late. This was obviously what the students wanted. He also made an important decision: since they had been working late, and would always open late from now on, and since Terry had to come in early to prepare the sauces, chop onions and grate the cheese, wouldn't it make sense he said (cautiously, almost despite himself, feeling that in the restaurant trade this might be opening the door to disaster) if Terry moved into the spare room?

Two days later Terry arrived with an old sports bag full of tapes, a ghetto blaster, and a black plastic rubbish sack bursting with t-shirts. He was there, on and off, for nearly five years.

An interlude: the sorbet

Those first years in Manchester were a whirlwind. Dr Nizami seemed to have no time to himself, in fact seemed never to leave the Casa Bolognese. His entire life was packed as tightly as one of Terry's cannelloni. About nine each morning he and Terry would meet in the kitchen. Dr Nizami would have strong English tea; Terry had instant coffee. Sometimes a late Saturday night shift meant Gaz couldn't make it to his bus to Northenden and would stay over with Terry. Sometimes (this puzzled Dr Nazimi) Gaz trotted out of Terry's room in his football shorts to collect two mugs of Maxwell House. Eventually this seemed to happen every morning, whether or not Gaz had a late shift, and even on days when he wasn't working at all. For the rest of the day Dr Nizami talked to suppliers or cashed-up at the bar, whilst Terry and Gaz, playing Terry's tapes, worked in the kitchen. At four o'clock all the staff would eat, and then at five they unbolted the front door. Time passed in a hectic noisy blur until midnight. This, or something like it, was the pattern six and a half days a week. On Sunday evenings the restaurant closed and Dr Nizami had a long bath (with jasmine oil) and then, wrapped in a towelling dressing gown, drank tea and set himself chess puzzles. These Sunday evenings excepted, Dr Nizami's time was so full of people, and so crowded with comings and goings, that it was almost a shock to realise one morning as he counted coins into piles, that he had no idea where his wife was these days.

The truth was that marriage had never meant much to Dr Nizami. It was just something that happened when he was younger, something he thought of in much the same category as the appearance of pubic hair or sitting his school exams. Of course it made his parents happy and for a while he was interested in Mrs Nizami but only, he thought now, as a kind of expensive pet. He studied and worked on his doctorate and she — she did what? — it was a mystery, and since they hardly ever spoke it was a mystery he still couldn't solve. His brother had mentioned her from time to time in his twice-yearly letters. Mostly, it seemed, she was living in her parents' huge apartment in Kuwait City, studying law and working hard. Perhaps she had qualified as an attorney by now?

Secondi Piatto

Success breeds success and soon an assistant chef was employed at Casa Bolognese. Terry was now able to escape from the restaurant from time to time: at first it was for an occasional midweek evening taking Gaz with him, but more often Terry went alone declaring with a laugh and using a phrase Dr Nizami found difficult to interpret, that Gaz was no longer "match fit." In theory Terry's absences were fine, but in fact Dr. Nizami slightly resented these evenings because he didn't get on well with the assistant chef, and had to explain things, which was irritating. Terry would come back late, breathing cigarettes and drink, and sometimes he didn't come back at all, appearing late the following morning smelling stale and airless, like an ill-ventilated bedroom. The nuisance caused by these absences entirely eclipsed any curiosity Dr Nizami might or might not have felt about Terry's whereabouts or companions. And, after all, it was none of his business. They may have shared a flat for years but apart from bleary meetings in the kitchen their long working hours meant the space for genuine sociability was strictly limited.

Perhaps two months after the assistant chef arrived — and after a sequence of enigmatic mid-morning re-appearances — Terry announced that Gaz wouldn't be working at the restaurant any more and that he, Terry, would like to take the weekend as holiday, if that was ok. He planned to stay with a friend in London. Dr Nizami was naturally concerned. He was not at all sure that cover could be arranged and only agreed with many hesitations and much reluctance. Somewhere he was conscious that besides making his life more complicated the London trip was significant for Terry and so, in a strange way, for himself. And these thoughts, in so far as they were thoughts, mixed with fear that Casa Bolognese was about to lose its principal asset, which was its chef. If he hadn't been preoccupied with rotas, and with preparing for the freezer as many batches of lasagne as Terry could produce, Dr Nizami might have stopped to examine these glimmerings. But he didn't.

Dr Nizami's worst fears were, in any case, realised. One weekend's leave-of-absence turned into another, taken at short notice a month later, and there was a third soon after that. Before long Terry was away more weekends than he was on the premises. To the customers nothing seemed to change but Dr Nizami was anxious and unhappy.

That was in June, and Dr Nizami's misery continued through 1995. But in January 1996 Terry took just one weekend trip to London, and in February none at all. Dr Nizami was naturally delighted even if he was sensitive enough to keep the delight to himself. Yet Dr Nizami noticed that the return to the old routine did not seem to be making Terry happy. Always a neat and self-contained lodger, Terry now slammed doors and forgot to wash up. He seemed to lose interest in the restaurant. For a week he was taciturn in the kitchen and, after shifts, spent a lot of time playing loud music in his room. Dr Nizami was worried.

The next morning, Terry announced that he was leaving. He had been offered a good job in the restaurant at a big new city centre hotel and it was an opportunity too good to turn down. Dr Nizami understood that he couldn't hang onto a good chef for ever — he had been half expecting this for years — and honourably declared he would not stand in Terry's way. They had done so much together — building Casa Bolognese from nothing into an institution — it had been good — he was grateful — and they hugged uncomfortably. At least, Dr Nizami felt uncomfortable. A few days later Terry was gone, taking his old sports bag (now full of CDs, not tapes), and leaving the spare room as empty as he found it.

Dolce

Twelve months later and another intake of students had began to discover the conveniences and comforts of dining with Gino at the Casa Bolognese. The assistant chef was now the chef — the new Terry — although Dr Nazimi had not offered him Terry's old room, nor would he. Dr Nizami still helped out downstairs. Some of the regular customers made a point of having a few words with 'Gino' — and if they did he smiled, and shook their hand, and said with gusto "and how are you, my friend?" — but he tended to spend most of his evenings between the kitchen, which needed close supervision, and his sitting room, where he watched TV news and documentaries.

It was one October evening in 1997 as Dr Nizami was watching the News at Ten (tension between America and Iraq was mounting, and that worried Dr Nizami very much) that the telephone rang. He answered with reluctance, still watching the television, assuming it would be a waitress resigning — that kind of call tended to come late at night. Instead he heard a man's voice, and the man was asking if he could speak to Terry. Dr Nizami explained that Terry had moved out a year or more ago and the man on the other end of the phone seemed surprised, perhaps even disappointed, and asked if Dr. Nizami had his new number. He didn't — it had never occurred to him before, but now it seemed rather odd to have no contact details. After a moment's thought he remembered the name of the hotel where Terry was working, and suggested the caller try there instead. The call ended with polite apologies on both sides: the caller for being a nuisance, and Dr Nizami for not being able to be more helpful.

A week later the man called again. It seemed that Terry was no longer at the hotel — it had proved impossible to track him down — and the caller said he guessed, since Terry had lived with Dr Nizami for so long, that he might like to know this. Dr Nizami said he appreciated the thought and was surprised Terry had moved. Terry was such a loyal man — and so hard working, and the man on the telephone agreed. Terry was indeed very loyal, the man said, it was one of his most conspicuous traits, almost as conspicuous as the tattoos. Dr Nizami laughed and feeling slightly nostalgic said "City Forever" in a bad Manchester accent. Dr Nizami laughed again, and the man laughed, too. The call ended with more apologies: the man for interrupting Dr Nizami's evening, and Dr Nizami for — well, he did not know what for.

A fortnight passed before the next call. The man said he wondered if Terry had been in touch with Dr. Nizami? Dr Nizami said no, sadly he hadn't, and then there was a pause and the man said, it was five years wasn't it? Dr Nizami was confused for a moment, because he had been in Manchester for seven years — he was very proud of this number, and told people as often as possible — so it took him a short time to realise that the man was still talking about Terry. Yes, he said, five years, almost exactly. Do you miss him, the man asked. I suppose I do, said Dr Nizami, and in his mind a parade of well-made pasta dishes marched past, each glossier and redder and more successful than the one before. I missed him for a while, too, said the man before adding briskly, but we only made it to eighteen months. Well, must get on, the man said. This time the call ended with no apologies.

The following evening there was another call, but this one was different. There were no hesitant introductions and no questions about Terry. Look, said the man, this is silly. We keep talking and you don't even know my name. I'm Robert. Hello, said Dr Nizami, I'm Dr Nizami. I know, said the man, Terry told me all about you when he came down to London. All about me, said Dr Nizami, incredulous, but he doesn't really know me. Well, said the man, we shall see.

After that they spoke on the telephone at least once a week, sometimes more. Dr Nizami told him about the restaurant, and how he had come to Manchester, and they talked a lot about British news and current affairs which they both found fascinating and both treated as something strangely foreign and exotic. The contrasts between London and Manchester often got mentioned: they would each look out of the window and describe the weather, and inevitably this would end in more laughter. They even discussed pizzas, with Robert explaining what toppings were popular in the smart expensive pizzerias of the capital. He listed dishes loaded with goats-milk cheeses, anchovies, spinach, exotic sausages and capers, and Dr Nizami tut-tutted and said that such things would never sell profitably in Fallowfield. They also talked about Terry and it seemed Terry had in fact been very observant, because the man knew all about the Sunday evening chess puzzles, and the jasmine bath oil and also, surprisingly, about the long-forgotten wife. Dr Nizami had no idea anybody knew so much about him, or cared enough to notice and thinking this he remembered Terry with a new and puzzled warmth.

It seemed quite natural to both of them that, one day the following spring, the man should say to Dr Nizami: I would like to see this Fallowfield, where the students do not know the meaning of the word anchovy and give their hearts to the Casa Bolognese. And it seemed equally natural that Dr Nizami should agree.

Coffee and the bill

So there he is, Dr Nizami, standing as still as a pillar in the low-ceilinged dimly-lit fast-moving chaos of the old, unrefurbished, Piccadilly railway station. It is 3rd March 1998. It is nine o'clock in the evening. He is waiting. Waiting for what? Immediately, he is waiting for Robert, the man on the telephone, whose train is due any minute. More distantly, more metaphysically, he doesn't know what he is waiting for and has not stopped to ask. He is excited, he knows that, almost as excited as that day eight years ago when carrying a cardboard suitcase, a complicated passport and a great deal of hope, he followed the throng off a similar train and towards the taxi rank. From the concourse he can see, beyond the platforms and the trainshed, the gentle curve of parallel tracks which ultimately lead to London. The Intercity from Euston is due any moment and he feels strangely proud. Dr Nizami thinks: here, in this city of Manchester, I am the host, and he is the newcomer. For a moment holding this thought he is calm, but then he sees the distant white headlamp of a train and this triggers a small wave of anxiety: will this man from the telephone want to eat in the restaurant, rather than in the upstairs flat? The restaurant would be difficult: will I have to explain that my professional name is Gino? Will he find that strange? I could order a pizza — have a pizza sent up — that would be a solution. So Dr. Nizami's thoughts ran.

The soon-to-be-arrived train glimpsed a moment ago has now snaked across two sets of points and is heading towards the station. Others who, like him, are waiting for friends, or relatives, or lovers from London, are converging on the designated platform. Dr Nazimi feels his anxiety turning into panic. Why has he agreed to this foolishness? What terrible chaos — forgotten orders, miscalculated payments, dirty plates — will be breaking out back at Casa Bolognese, now that he's not there to supervise? And who is this man anyway, this man who is coming on the train from London specially to see him? Despite all those hours and all those evenings on the telephone, do they really have anything in common, except Terry? Does he really appreciate the dynamics of low budget student dining? The cosy intimacy of their voice-only relationship instantly feels thin, two-dimensional and above all, suspicious. At the back of his mind Dr Nizami is aware of irrational fears he cannot quieten: this man could be a murderer — or worse, a thief. For a moment Dr Nizami's panic is intense but it does not last because suddenly it is announced that the 21.03 from London Euston is arriving at platform six. This will

be it, this will be the man from the telephone, the man Terry....
Dr Nazimi's mind suddenly stumbles. The man Terry did what
with? It makes no sense. The train, its diesel engine
thundering, shudders to a halt just feet from the buffers; doors
are flung open; travelers spill out onto the platform pulling
little suitcases on wheels or hurrying for cabs. Somewhere in
that crowd is the man — the man? that word again — the man
he was waiting for. As a smiling face moves towards him it
seems to Dr Nizami that a chasm full of things he doesn't
understand has opened unexpectedly beneath him.

Have you ever eaten in Casa Bolognese? It is still there, I
believe. The red paper napkins, the laminated menu, the tank
of tropical fish, the rainbow flag outside — it is exactly like
every other cheap Italian restaurant in Manchester.
Well, almost.

Pancake Day

It was pancake day at the nudist club and nobody knew what to wear. Examining his face carefully in the shaving mirror and scraping away another band of stubble Roger says: "What if the fat splashes? Imagine that. It could be awful." Behind him in the bath, just visible in the fogged-up mirror, rolly-polly Martin replies: "Blemishes."

"Would an apron ....?" says Roger.

"I think not," says Martin, cutting in.

Scrape, scrape, more stubble is washed away.

Martin splish-splashes thoughtfully with his feet. "You know I don't think they're proper nudists at all," he says.

Roger turns and says: "How come?"

Martin replies: "All they want is groupsex." And he says it just like that. One word. Groupsex.

"They?" says Roger, "It's not as if we've been flooded with new members. There are only two."

Martin lets himself slide down into the water until it just laps his nostrils and completely covers his mouth. A reply is out of the question.

"It'll be good to meet new guys," says Roger. "I think I'll send them a text, make sure they're coming."

■

Martin is putting the last unused Bourbon Creams into a plastic box — the rest are arranged on a plate like spokes on a wheel — when he is interrupted by the door chime. He snaps the lid shut and looks up at the kitchen clock. Five to eleven. Someone is early. "Roger," he calls, then still holding the box he wobbles fleshily down the hall and calls up the stairs, "Roger, could you get the door. I've not found the shortbreads."

Behind the frosted glass of the front door a silhouetted visitor holding a briefcase shifts his weight from one foot to the other.

Upstairs there is movement — a door opens, a door shuts, then there is the hurried padding of heavy feet on carpet. Phud-phud, Phud-phud, Phud-phud and Roger appears at the bottom of the stairs.

"Will these do?" he says, in a stage whisper.

Martin's huge head appears round the kitchen door, he looks Roger up and down and then concentrates on the only item of clothing he is wearing: a pair of yellow beach-style flipflops.

"They'll have to," he says. "Now be a pet and let Gerry in."

■

By the time Jon finds Martin and Roger's semi-detached house in Walkden several others have arrived. He can hear them talking behind the discretely-curtained window against a gentle background of Radio 2. He presses the bell.

"Hello?" says Roger, only his head peering round the glass front door. It is perfectly obvious through the glass that he has nothing on. "Are you for the group?"

Jon nods.

"Then slide in, out of that cold, brrr," says Roger, stepping aside to let the new arrival into the overheated hall. "Glad you could come, Jon. Well look its all very simple. You can take your clothes off in the back bedroom. Just lay them on the bed," and he gestures up the bleakly carpeted stairs. At the top are two cheaply-framed prints of random muscular men. "Then come down for some coffee when you're ready, ok?"

Roger smiles a welcome then turns and opens the door into the front room from which leaks the mixed odours of a gas fire, condensation and Mellow Birds. Jon can just hear a few smothered "oohs?" and "who's that?" before it closes.

The conversation stops dead when Jon eventually walks in. All eyes turn on him. Martin separates himself from the beanbag upon which he's been lolling and stands up.

"Jon, we're so glad you could make it. Rupert was particularly glad to hear that you were coming because he comes from Bury, too," and he flutters his sausage fingers towards an exquisite childlike figure who appears to be made of porcelain.

Rupert, who looks to Jon like he is probably in his late thirties, lifts a flawless little arm in a sort of imperial greeting that might also be a blessing. "Prestwich," he says.

Martin continues: "And over there on the couch is Gerry."

Gerry, middle-aged, heavily-tanned and sagging, looks sheepishly down at the large and elaborate briefcase tucked protectively behind his hairy legs. Jon glances for a moment at the briefcase. Martin follows his eyes approvingly.

"Gerry is a businessman," Martin explains. "Now who else? That's Derek holding the mug." Derek, a wiry pensioner wearing only hiking boots and thick woolly socks, lifts his mug in a silent salute. "There's Roger of course, my other half. And finally," and he twists round to flash a smile at a youngish spindly man with a pudding-basin haircut and spectacles sitting upright on a borrowed dining room chair. The young man smiles weakly and confusedly as if everyone in the room were a participant in some odd nightmarish dream in which he discovered, midway through a job interview, that he didn't have any clothes on. "Mike," says the young man. "I'm in electrical retail. It's my first time too."

Martin indicates a place next to Rupert on the settee. "You can sit here, Jon, whilst Roger puts the kettle back on. Now," he says, "is everyone near a coaster?" Five heads look to left and right and then nod. "Gerry, could you give Rupert a hand with the tea?"

Gerry reluctantly stands, picks up his brief case and follows Roger out into the hall.

"Well this is nice," says Martin, settling himself back down on the beanbag which, taking his weight, strains all around him like a bloated buoyancy aid. "Jon, have you been a nudist for very long?"

Everyone looks at Jon.

"Nope. This is my first time."

"I see," says Martin. "Well, we're all very friendly here. No need to be shy."

Derek takes a swig from his mug.

"But this isn't really a dating agency, do you understand?" Martin says rather suddenly.

Rupert swivels his signet ring.

"It's not about s-e-x, see? It doesn't matter what you look like, prince charming or ugly frog, because when you've got no clothes on everyone's the same."

Martin smiles, fatly satisfied. Jon smiles back, noticing on the wall next to the television the framed photograph of two men in campy hired morning suits; Roger with a big purple bow-tie, Martin with a frilly lavender one, each holding a champagne flute and both looking shiny and sweating. Beneath, set into an oval cut out of the mount, it says: Together For Ever, June 2010.

Jon says: "Do you mean we're all guys sitting around with no clothes on, and nobody's meant to look at anyone else?"

"No no no no no," says Martin shaking his head. "You see..."

"So we can look, but mustn't think about what we see?"

"Jon it's nudism, about gay men being comfortable around other men. With no clothes on."

"Comfortable but not turned on?"

Martin mouths a frosty "Yes," then turns to Mike: "Sorry Mike, we were all forgetting you. Before Jon was so good as to join us you were telling everybody about the latest developments in save-to-disc video technology."

■

Gerry has put his briefcase down on the kitchen counter, and is now standing in front of it protectively.

"I don't need to tell you," Roger is telling him as he fills the kettle, "but it's not easy living with Martin. He's so jealous. So suspicious. Sometimes I wonder what I'm doing with him. After all, I'm GBFM."

Gerry looks blank.

"Good boy friend material. And a bloody good lay." He reaches into a cupboard and pulls out a ragged paper bag of sugar. "You had any good lays recently, Gerry?"

Gerry shrugs and looks embarrassed.

"Sly dog," says Roger. "I bet you have a great time. You single lads." He pours some of the sugar into a little sparkly glass bowl.

"I often wonder whether I should — you know — keep my hand in a bit more. Don't want to lose touch with the scene, after all. Do you know anyone who might fancy a shag, Gerry?"

Gerry, his eyes fixed on the floor, shakes his head.

"I bet you do," says Roger. He opens the fridge bending over in a way that forces his sun-bedded buttocks slightly apart, and which might have been deliberate. "That new bloke, Jon, is a bit tasty don't you think?" he says.

Gerry does not lift his eyes from the floor.

The kitchen door flies open and Martin enters at velocity: "Roger," he says. "Could I borrow you for a moment in the vestibule?"

.

Back in the living room Rupert is speaking so quietly the others can barely hear him over the hiss of the gas fire.

"It was so much worse before Roger moved in, so much worse," he says. "We had to bring towels."

Jon's eyes widened in disbelief. "Sheesh," he says.

"But it's true," says Rupert, and Derek looked his agreement. "We had to sit on the towels. So we didn't spoil the upholstery."

The raised voices of a disagreement filter through from the hall. Roger is loudly protesting "But you said I could?" but Martin's replies are not clear.

"As if this," says Rupert, waving at the dowdy brown velour suite, "as if this needed protecting."

Jon scratches his balls thoughtfully.

"So, Jesus, what do you talk about?" says Jon.

"Television. Jobs. It was like visiting an aunt. Hardly fun, but if you want to mix...." says Rupert. "There are dozens of guys who take an interest. But Martin won't let any new members join. He vets them. Says they would say they were going for a piss, sneak up to the bedroom, and steal our credit cards. You know that you and Mike are only here because Roger insisted," then widening his eyes: "Insisted."

From the hall it is clear that Roger and Martin's row has reached its muffled climax.

"Well, fuck you," Roger barks and then phud phud phud they hear him flip-flop up the stairs and bolt himself in the bathroom.

The entire house is silent. Rupert begins mouthing a countdown: one, two, three and by the time he reaches eight Martin, bigger and pinker than ever, re-appears in the living room.

"I'm going to start making the batter," he says with assumed brightness. "Now who wants pancakes?"

.

Everyone troops into the kitchen and Gerry hands round the mugs of tea, then they all watch whilst Martin cracks six eggs into a basin. Occasionally there is the scuffy sound of bare feet on vinyl kitchen flooring.

"I'm not bothering with free range," Martin loudly confides to Derek, who is standing closest. "But I have got a few little luxuries up my sleeve," and he points his eggy fork at the counter where a miniature bottle of Drambuie and a pack of supermarket butter are displayed.

Jon, who is last into the kitchen and standing closest to the door, turns to Mike, who is next to him, and says: "So, you do any sport?"

Mike affects a polite reluctance to drag his eyes from the cookery exhibition. "Swimming," he says before adding thoughtfully: "You know."

"They have men-only nude swimming sessions in London," says Jon.

Mike is about to reply but before he can do so Martin intervenes. "The trick," he announces, now working the mixture vigorously, "is to use a wooden spoon."

For the next few minutes there is silence broken only by the sound of batter forming until, directly above them, there is a thundering noise. It carries on at a steady even rate for a sufficiently masculine length of time then there is the sound of a toilet flushing, followed soon after by a cough.

"I hope he's got that window open," says Martin. "I can't stand the smell of cigarette smoke in the bathroom. There," he says, showing the basin triumphantly. "We're ready to fry."

■

It was agreed that they would take plates and forks back into the sitting room and wait for Martin to serve up. Mike would stay to help him with lemons and sugar.

Derek, Jon and Rupert sit on the settee, naked thigh squeezed against naked thigh, a cold plate on each lap, whilst Gerry opts for Mike's borrowed dinning room chair, carefully placing his briefcase beside it.

"Four years ago?" says Rupert and he turns to Derek for confirmation. "We started with a nude dinner party. Napkins, candles on the table. It all felt rather naughty. Roger wore white cuffs. Just white cuffs. A few months later Derek bought Gerry along, so then there were five of us round the table."

A floorboard creaks somewhere above them.

"I think Roger was rather hoping today would be the beginning of something new," he says and then whispers, with a cautious glance at the kitchen door beyond which hot fat can be heard to sizzle furiously, "An open relationship."

"And so I'm allowed to join the group?" Jon says.

"Yes, you and Mike. One for each of them. Mike was for Martin."

Derek crosses his legs in a manly ankle-on-knee manner and begins to study the complicated weltings and lacings of his elaborately high-tech boots.

"And Martin knows about this plan?" says Jon.

Rupert shrugs. "Probably," he says.

As they talk Gerry silently hauls his briefcase up on to his lap, opens it, and begins to explore inside, the case folding down onto his neck as if he has placed his head into a set of outsize fake-leather jaws. Jon and Rupert stare at him.

"Roger's making a hell of a lot of assumptions," says Jon, still watching the half-devoured Gerry.

"I think it was all rather aspirational," says Rupert, his eyes also fixed on Gerry.

The smell of burning and the sound of catastrophe coming from the kitchen is, by this stage, difficult to ignore. A crashing of metallic objects and a shriek of pain are followed by Mike's sudden explosion into the sitting room. His right leg and most of his chest are covered in a series of screaming red splashes.

"He's mad," cried Mike, flapping at his skin in an effort cool it. "He tried to pour hot butter on my dick." Immediately there is an ominous roaring-sound from the kitchen and the burning smell turns acrid. Smoke alarms are activated to produce a violent electronic pulse. There is a scream from the kitchen and the crunch of breaking glass. "Silly bloody queen," Roger shouts as he thunders down the stairs and charges along the hall. "Silly. Bloody. Queen."

"I didn't mean…" Martin is heard to say, as Roger flings open the kitchen door, "It was the Drambuie." Then the kitchen door slams shut. Over the shouted accusations and high-volume counter-accusations the nudists in the sitting room can hear the back door opening and the sound of a frying pan hitting a patio-like object.

Jon stands up but Derek waves him back to his seat.

Rupert says to Mike: "You'd better go and splash some water on that."

The kitchen door flies open and Martin bolts passed them and out into the hall, a fleshy ball of tears.

In the midst of the chaos nobody has noticed that Gerry has finished rummaging in his briefcase. He has retrieved whatever he was after, and is now standing proud and motionless in front of them, legs slightly apart, chin high, hands on his hips like a model from an Amateur Physique magazine of the 1950s. He is smiling ineffably.

All eyes turn to examine him.

"Gerry dear," says Rupert. "Wherever did you get that fabulous cock ring?"

The Posh Bit of Stockport

He said the Plough. I said the Elizabethan. We went to the Plough.

At least let's try Town Bar, I said, as we walked down Heaton Moor Road. You know, young, trendy, cool, like you're supposed to be? But Adam said: no, it's good to keep in touch with his roots. Chas had said that was important.

Chas is his agent. Everything that Chas says is right. Apparently.

The Plough was like it always is, and always has been, and will always be. It is the place in Heaton Moor that is least like the rest of Heaton Moor. It is not smart. No Hollister, no SuperDry or Diesel, no Abercrombie & Fitch, but lots of Next and a little bit of Primark. It smelled of scampi and chips. Adam went straight to the bar, gave the big shouldered girl behind it the cheeky-lad smile, the smile for which he is famous, and ordered two pints of Stella. I left him to it and found a table at the back, away from the videos, somewhere we could have a bit of peace.

I suppose it was a normal Friday night in The Plough. Lads playing pool at the back, a non-descript match on the big screen, couples of various ages eating bar meals, him with a pint, her with a glass of white wine. Every single person in The Plough has heard Adam's name, could tell you the back-story of his character in intimate detail, and would instantly recognise him in the celebrity gossip pages of TV Quick ("Out clubbing with girlfriend Stacey Ashton: 'We've been together three months and we're still totally loved-up,' said Adam" or "Adam glimpsed training for next week's charity football match"). Yet there's nothing special about him. Nice boyish face, neat build, but put him in an ordinary Stockport pub like this and he's Mr Ordinary Stockport Lad, anonymous apart from the perfectly laundered looks. Soap star: there's a clue in the name.

Weird vibe, he said when he eventually sat down. No, I said, for these people you're the weird one. And he was. Dressed in classic jeans paired with a simple two-button jacket, expensive t-shirt (acid yellow, with CTRL ALT DELETE printed on it in big black capitals), box fresh white trainers, he just looked so much better than anyone else. Cleaner, shinier, faultless. Like something off the TV — which, of course, he is.

No mate, really weird, he said, leaning forward. Not just normal weird, but seriously screwed up. That girl behind the bar? Says she's my cousin Liam's girlfriend's sister.

He took a big gulp of his pint. She's a bit rough, he said, and flashed one of those smiles at me. I really don't think he knows when he's doing it.

It was your idea to get back to your roots, I said. You went to school with half of them.

Yup, he said. Chilling with my people. Feels good.

Good not weird? I asked.

Don't, he said. You know what I mean. And he smiled again and looked around, probably to see if anyone had noticed him. They had, of course. It's not that he's vain — no more vain than anyone else in his position — it's just how he deals with the world. Always thinking about his audience.

I shouldn't be on the beer, he said, drinking, and he mentioned the name of one of the fashionable party nights, the kind with a guest list and a following among the beautiful people of Manchester: Jason, Ferdy and Luke, Danny, Gary and Ryan, all of them footballers or stars from rival soaps, or club promoters, off-duty DJs, or the playboy owners of chains of Salford tanning salons. He was there until late, with Stacey.

Woke up as rough as a Brillo, he said. Still drinking, he looks over my shoulder at the pool tables. For a moment I catch him scanning the players, four lads whose four girlfriends were sitting at the table beside us. A quick glance up and down, almost furtive. He's measuring himself against them, but not to check that he's better off, better looking and better dressed (he knows that) but to check that he hasn't strayed too far from the local norm. That he's still one of them, underneath.

A fiver says if I bought one of them a pint it'd get in the papers, he said. Then, looking at me again: Chas says I've got to keep in with the fan base. Follow a few randoms on Twitter. You know the game.

He picked up his pint, brought it to his lips, then paused. I was necking it all day yesterday, he said. Waster, aren't I?

Actually a waster is something Adam has never been. He's a hard worker, very focused. Homework was always completed on time, enthusiastic with the after-school clubs, football in winter, cricket in the summer. And those stage-school sessions on Saturdays. I always told his parents: a high achiever, made for success.

Then it all came out, the reason why he wanted to talk to me.

The day before Chas took him for a long lunch, to catch up, he'd said. Chas told him he'd lined up a part in a TV mini-series. Just the kind of move you should make, he told Adam. Broaden your credits, move out of the soap silo. It would be a prison drama, gritty stuff, Adam would play Kev, the new boy, learning the ropes, surviving and then thriving inside. Star billing, Chas said, and he mentioned who was being queued for the warder, for the old lag, for the best mate, for the prison's Mr Big. It sounded good.

Adam was keen: great, I'm up for it, he'd said, bring it on. But as they finished the second bottle of Pinot Grigio Chas told him the USP: Kev was gay.

So, said Adam, looking at me. What do you think?

Can you do it? I asked.

Adam frowned. Duh, he said, of course.

He took another gulp from his pint and looked over my shoulder. Behind me I could hear the pool lads getting excited. You gimp, one shouted, and they all laughed. They had Adam's full attention, but he reluctantly turned back to me. That smile again.

Bit of snogging, he said, few scenes with my shirt off. Nothing I can't handle. Kev's fit. Toned. Spends a lot of time in the prison gym. Chas said there's lots of banter over the weights. Tidy bloke. He says it's a big marketing opportunity playing a gay lad.

He was still talking but I don't remember what because I'd been snagged by what he'd just said. Funny, I thought, how he emphasises the body. Young man's pride. And as I thought this an expression must have drifted across my face — he realised I wasn't listening — and stopped speaking.

You don't think I get it, do you, he said. The gay thing.

I said I was sure he'd do a good job.

The History Boys, he said. It blew me away. Best English class you ever taught.

I said: I thought *The View from the Bridge* was top of your reading list?

That too, he said. He smiled.

Adam slid his glass around the tabletop, as if he were writing something in the puddle of condensation left by his cold lager. He watched as the puddle swirled and stretched then separated into individual beads of water. Suddenly he seemed very young.

He's a dancer, he said. Kev's a dancer. What do I know about dancing?

Where's the problem, I asked. You don't actually have to dance, do you, not in prison?

Adam slid the glass around once again, breaking up the old beads and forming new ones.

Nope, he said watching the glass's progress. When I dance, I look like I'm kaylied.

For a moment we are both silent, together in the noisy bar. It's a bit like the old days. Have we reached a full-stop? Or is he asking for my advice? We sit uncomfortably in the space between these two possibilities, Adam reading the runes he has written on the table, and me watching Adam.

It's just the dance that bothers you? I ask.

He nods. Then shakes his head.

Kev's just a bit. A bit camp. And he said "camp" under his breath, almost a whisper, like it was a dirty word. I don't know, he said. It just feels. Chas is well-in with this producer guy. He said if I bottle it.

Adam didn't finish the sentence. For a moment he looked straight at me with those famous eyes.

Then he said: Chas said it didn't do Daniel Day-Lewis any harm.

I wonder for a moment if he knows who Daniel Day-Lewis is. Why should he? He's only nineteen, and *My Beautiful Laundrette* was made six years before he was born. He finishes his pint.

And Johnny Lee Miller, Adam said, didn't stop him nailing Angelina Jolie.

This sounds exactly like a Chas line: up beat, optimistic, baited.

But they're divorced now, I said. And anyway, they both played the butch parts. Did Chas mention James Wilby from *Maurice?* We didn't see him for years. And Glen Berry from *Beautiful Thing*. Hardly a big career break.

For a moment he looked quizzical, then: I get what you're doing, he said. Wind-up merchant. He nudges his empty glass towards me. Your turn, he said.

By now the pub was crowded, and as I stood waiting to be served I wondered what exactly Adam's problem was, and why he felt he needed to talk to me. Eighteen months ago, when he was doing bit-parts in *Skins* and *Waterloo Road* and hanging around in the background in coffee bar scenes in Hollyoaks, it used to be easy to read him. He was on the way up, and enjoying it. But now? Eventually my turn came and the big-shouldered barmaid, the girlfriend of Adam's cousin Liam, took my order. She wasn't at all rough, on the contrary she was rather well spoken. She was certainly very polite.

I got back to our table to find Adam's jacket hanging over the back of his chair, but Adam himself gone. It only took a few moments to spot him — in fact, I heard him first. He was with the pool lads. No problem, any time pal, he was saying to one of them as he autographed a beer mat. Then another of them offered him a cue, and he positioned himself for what looked like a very professional shot. For a while I nursed my drink in silence, preferring not to disturb him. Is it wrong to say I enjoyed watching Adam playing at being one of the lads, playing the part he has chosen, easily and confidently and beautifully? I wouldn't be alone if I did. The ratings prove it.

The pool game seemed to be going well, so I decided that I'd probably performed whatever task it was Adam had in mind when he asked me out. He looked happy, content even, and I didn't mind being forgotten. I stood and ostentatiously played with my car keys and eventually Adam noticed me. He waved, but did not interrupt the game. Bell me, he shouted, and gave me a thumbs up.

For a moment I thought about walking round to his parents house to say hello — very nice people, lawyers both of them, we used to be on the PTA committee together. It's only a few hundred yards away from the Plough, a very handsome Edwardian place facing the park. But in the end that seemed rather intrusive.

Tea at the Rectory

Over at the rectory bath-time was just an expensively fragranced memory. Lolling on a Pompadour print sofa and bathed in the gentle cream light of silk-shaded lamps, was a slight but exquisitely dressed man. Licking a flawless index finger he slowly turned the pages of a glossy interiors magazine. As he did so an episcopal-looking ring on his second finger cast a sudden, dazzling beam. Around him china dogs, chenille throws, and gilt chairs flashed their naked opulence. He flashed his back.

It wasn't long before the telephone rang. A languid hand reached out and answered.

There was a pause.

"No," he said.

There was another pause.

"No," he said.

"Well I shall try," he said, then added after a momentary pause, "Bless you," and put the receiver back down.

It really was terrifically trying: instead of four for supper, there would be five. Graham, it seemed, would be bringing a friend. He reached once again for the telephone. With his eyes shut as if prepared for pain he listened to the dialing tone.

"We will be five tonight," he announced when at last the phone was answered.

"Yes, five. One extra," he said.

"Well get some more then," he said.

"How would I know?" he said.

"Yes, five," he said, his voice now steely. "You will sort it out. You always do. Goodbye mother." End of call.

Opposite, on the mirror-black lid of a grand piano, a Louis XVI clock delicately chimed the hour. He closed his eyes and retreated inside himself to that private, perfect space which is the fountain-head of poise: in his mind's eye the suburbs strung out along the A56 Bury New Road dissolved and were replaced by a sort of *Country Life* in which every house was a charming rectory and every proud owner a handsomely beneficed clergyman.

Father Bird opened his eyes to hear the clock chime the quarter-hour. Time to get ready. He swung himself upright, yawned, stretched his legs and turning his feet this way and that admired the soft golden doe-skin of his superbly comfortable Venetian slippers. "Duty calls," he said, and standing trotted into the hall, took two tiny paces across it, and opened the discrete panelled door that connected, via a short corridor painted a chillingly drab sage green, with the church. In the vestry Father Bird opened one of several horrid bookcases and ran his finger along the faded spines. *Commentaries on*

Leviticus should do nicely. Armed with the book and a pencil he arranged himself in a confessional box and, pretending to read, waited for the afternoon's visitors. Where the page ought to have been he saw a queue of badly-dressed people; people who, perching provisionally on the edge of their seat, would explain in clichés how they or their spouses were having affairs or telling lies or marrying for the wrong reasons or suddenly giving birth or failing to marry but giving birth all the same, all wearyingly commonplace events which he guessed the moment he heard their boring grey voices, but which they, carelessly, seemed never to have expected. Yet by the time the brass rings on the confessional curtain announced the first penitent his India-rubber nature had recovered its bounce so that as he closed his book he found himself thinking, with a thrill of anticipation, of the glittering evening ahead.

.

The food (and Father Bird's mother) arrived from Crumpsall at about six, Mrs Bird letting herself in with her own key. She stowed Delia's luxury fish pie in a warm oven, along with the steamed vegetables covered in foil. Starters she placed ready on the counter under clingfilm, cheese likewise. It took another few minutes for her to collect the dirty laundry from the basket in the bathroom, another minute or two to replace the guest soap and hand towel in the cloakroom downstairs, and then she was gone, locking the backdoor after her.

All this time Father Bird was in his bedroom. A vast piece of rich honey-colour Edwardian woodwork stood at the far end. This monument to a more generous age enjoyed twin functions: first, it stored socks, underwear and collars; second, it allowed Father Bird to say, as he often did, how much he appreciated a tallboy within reach of his bed. A full-length

mirror completed the scene of gentlemanly order. Father Bird —
already wearing a pair of well-made black trousers and a
fetchingly casual shirt — examined his reflection. He judged it
satisfactory. Selecting a handsome tweed jacket threaded with
green and yellow, and a Prussian blue silk handkerchief for the
breast pocket, he gave himself a final approving inspection
before strolling downstairs to re-arrange the silverware.

Magnus and Toby were first to arrive as usual, chattering and
bickering happily, then came Graham, throwing out extravagant
compliments about Father Bird's sublime handkerchief and
instantly noticing everything: not a single repositioned
photographed or recently acquired cushion escaping either his
attention or his comment. Tagging on behind, surfing the
slipstream of Graham's torrent of high-achieving adjectives,
was the surprise fifth guest, a silent smiling student introduced
as William.

It was as the last of the wine was emptied into Magnus' lead-
crystal glass and Graham, dabbing up crumbs of Stilton,
declared with a smile that the meal had been another of Father
Bird's *cuisines superbes,* that attention turned to William.

"You are at university then, William," said Father Bird adding,
with what he took to be a becomingly antique turn of phrase:
"What are you reading?"

"Economics, mostly" said William.

"Doesn't that sound clever?" said Graham. "He's explained
inelasticity of demand to me several dozens of times but I just
can't get it. I hear the words but see bulging lycra."

All tittered appreciatively.

"And what do you do when you are not reading economics, William? Do you play rugby?" said Father Bird, treating 'rugby' as if it were a rather thrillingly dirty word.

"Rugby, sometimes," said William non-committally. All leaned forward just perceptibly. "But I don't play any more. It's my back."

"So it's been a life crowded with incident, then?" said Father Bird, getting into his stride. "Oh you know," said William. "This and that."

"William is very active," said Graham.

"I bet you are. A big strong boy like you," said Father Bird.

"And he is very popular," said Graham.

"Naturally. If he's active," said Father Bird.

"In fact he's just getting over a little tendresse, which is why I thought it might be fun if he came along this evening. A change being as good as a rest."

"Bless you," said Father Bird. "Shall we all retire to the drawing room?"

Later, sitting side by side on the sofa, Father Bird said to William: "Seriously now, what do you do when you're not writing clever essays?"

"All kinds of things," said William. Then, having glanced around the room: "That's a very grand piano you have there."

"It is indeed," said Father Bird. "Are you musical?"

"Very musical," said William. "I have pianists' hands," and he held them up.

Father Bird allowed himself a little theatrical gasp.

"Do you play often?" he asked.

"As often as I can."

"You must touch my keys," said Father Bird.

They were silent for a moment, a conversational plateau having been reached. Then William said: "I like the way you've done this place. Very Petit Trianon meets the late Queen Mother." And although Father Bird suspected that William was indebted to Graham for the aperçu — and made a mental note to tax him about it later — he felt himself strangely charmed.

Graham telephoned the following morning, Father Bird deciding to take the call in the Turkish splendour of his bedroom because his mother was downstairs clearing up after the night before and he found her noise intolerable.

"Well," said Graham, "what did you think of him?"

Father Bird conceded that William was a very personable young man.

"He's gorgeous," corrected Graham. "He's also very clever and interesting but he was *un peu timide* last night. Overawed by our brilliance, I expect. But he opened up in the cab —"

Father Bird began to say something but thought better of it.

" — and he talked about your piano non-stop. He's dying to meet you again."

And as Father Bird went about the urgent business of the day — selecting new curtains for the spare room, speaking to the churchwardens about long meditated changes to the flower rota — he couldn't help feeling that it would be nice to meet young William once more.

.

Their first date was tea at the rectory. It had been agreed through Graham: William would call round to borrow some sheet music from Father Bird's collection — a little Lehár, some Irving Berlin, a few Chopin Polonaises. There would be cake and a pot of Darjeeling and William would be gone by three so that Father Bird could be ready to lead his Thursday evening marriage preparation class.

William was punctual, which was a strong point in his favour, and clearly very much more relaxed this time. He was charming and winningly boyish about how much he liked the Victoria sponge and when Father Bird happened to mention the difficulty of finding reliable organists he volunteered his long interest in church music and asked intelligently about the services. When William finished his tea he carefully placed his cup and saucer on the side table, nestling it amongst the framed photographs of actresses and archbishops (all signed) without causing them the least disturbance. Father Bird noted this with approval, as he also noted William's expensively understated blue shirt (Thomas Pink, he guessed) and his brogues (definitely Tricker). When the time came to leave and Father Bird, standing by the front door held out his hand and said: "It has been a splendid afternoon" William hesitated for a moment then gave him a hug and a little peck on the cheek. It was all most satisfactory.

Thereafter things moved rapidly. William telephoned on Sunday evening to say thank you for the scores and they talked for ages, Father Bird saying mischievous things about the old ladies on the parochial church council and William egging him on. The following week they spoke several more times and on Friday — Father Bird being obliged to call in at the Diocesan office on a point of detail about his pension — they met by appointment at a coffee bar off Deansgate, and each had lattes and whispered about the other customers, and laughed a lot.

A few days later William dropped in, as if by accident. This time they had gins and tonic and talked about the relationship of music, ornament and liturgy, then about whether either of them could ever sleep with what Father Bird called a woman of the female persuasion (they couldn't, unless the circumstances were exceptional) and before he left William borrowed the scores to *Oklahoma* and a batch of Lizst's *Hungarian Rhapsodies*. Much later that night, humming 'I'm just a girl who can't say no', Father Bird switched off the drawing room's silk-shaded lamps one by one with even more satisfaction than usual.

■

William's visits to the rectory increased in both frequency and duration: despite the deterrently awful cross-city bus journeys, weekly turned into daily, afternoons into evenings and, ultimately, evenings into mornings. As Father Bird explained to Graham it was the smoothest seduction there had ever been, so much so that he wasn't at all clear who had seduced whom. Later that day, motoring back from a cremation in Bolton with the undertakers fee fat in his wallet, Father Bird decided that he would buy William a little present, something delightful and handsome. An hour later, having detoured to a jewelers in

St Ann's Square, he was heading south to make his first call at William's Wilmslow Road hall of residence with an enchanting pair of cufflinks.

Father Bird, in dog collar and black jacket, parked his smart little car behind the Whitworth Art Gallery and walked the few yards to William's flat. First impressions were not encouraging: the architecture — a series of oversized red-brick chalets squeezed behind prison-like metal fencing — filled him with a depressing sense of the gracelessness of modern life. For the sake of William he decided to ignore it. He found the flat, rang the bell, and waited. According to the girl who answered William had gone out to buy some cigarettes, so Father Bird said he would wait in William's room.

The room was much like any other: white-washed brick walls, a few utilitarian pieces of cheaply blonde furniture, a computer, a single bed and an easy chair covered in cast-off clothes. As for beautification, efforts were scanty: there was a large black-and-white photograph of a jowly Evelyn Waugh, but that was it. All was pervaded by the strong smell of boy and the faint smell of Roger et Gallet soap, both of which met with his approval. Savouring the atmosphere Father Bird examined himself in the one really interesting piece of furniture — the mirror — then sat neatly on the bed to await his lover's return. It was five or ten minutes before he realised that the one thing he couldn't see among the student debris were the many scores he'd lent.

"I've brought something wicked," said Father Bird as he handed over the small silk-lined box.

"I hope this was very expensive," said William. The cufflinks were tried on, and they were judged to be extremely attractive in a man-about-town way. Excited and delighted, Father Bird said: "How do you think those cufflinks would look performing an arpeggio? There's a lovely little four-handed sonata by Mozart in one of those scores. Shall we try it? Do you have the score I lent you?"

As Father Bird later confessed to Graham, he knew the happiness could not last because then, bit by bit, it all came out: the scores were not there because they had been sold on Ebay, and it was not clear that William could even play the piano. References to evenings spent toying with an uncle's electric organ were deferentially offered and brusquely thrust aside, and it was a mark of the seriousness of the occasion that nobody bothered with the obvious double entendres. Now, his eyes opened, Father Bird recalled that he was missing a silver-framed photograph of Princess Marina, an ivory elephant, and a tiepin with a St George's flag motif. He'd blamed his mother — proverbially careless, you had to watch her constantly — but now he wasn't so sure. Was it possible? William threw himself on Father Bird's mercy: he was heavily in debt, he could barely afford to eat, his parents lived in a bungalow near Scarborough and they either couldn't or wouldn't help. He felt bad — no, awful — and he could not hope to be forgiven, but visiting Father Bird had been an escape into a new and better world. How bitterly he now regretted his behaviour, especially since last night, the night when their affair ceased to be a game and had become, he swore, very real.

Furious and hurt Father Bird drove back to the northern suburbs in silence and at speed, the determination to be severe keeping his foot on the accelerator all the way from Rusholme. Arriving at the rectory he angrily told his mother — who was ironing a huge pile of shirts in the kitchen — not to bother him, not for any reason. She could let herself out when she'd finished. He'd had a trying day and was jaded. He was going to lie down.

Flat on his back on his oriental bedspread, hands clasped on his chest like a pious and well-dressed corpse, Father Bird fell asleep. When he awoke, a little refreshed, and once again in possession of his dignity, he resolved to consider the ups and downs of the day as he would other important issues — like selecting from a series of wallpaper samples or the vexed question of tie-backs. How does this fit my life, how does this suit my home? What does it say about me? Will it co-ordinate? The answers were all one way. He remembered the poster of Waugh on that dreary white brick wall. Poor lamb, he said to himself, he just wants to get on in life, to escape from his suburban hell. He is young and beautiful and how very much like me he is, and at this thought Father Bird's heart began to melt. William looked so good in the rectory — graced the chairs, improved the curtains — he was ornamental and as an accessory he could not be faulted. Father Bird's decision was all but made by the time he remembered that William's parents lived in a bungalow. Horrid — what torture — how brutal parents can be. There was only one solution: he would practice Christian forgiveness, and William would move into the rectory.

.

And so, six months later, another dinner party begins to assemble. From upstairs Father Bird hears the doorbell and William answer it. Magnus and Toby, first as usual. Catching himself in the mirror Father Bird can't avoid remarking that he is flushed and hot and not at all relaxed, and fiddling with his cufflinks (one falls to the floor, damn) he feels himself grow testy. But he will conquer this feeling because however much he hates being so far behind with his toilette, he knows he has no choice: how could he have had his bath sooner, when he had the chicken liver parfait to prepare? Of course this was never a problem when his mother did the cooking, but those days are long gone. William had said: "We don't need that old lady snooping around our house, do we? And her food is so boring anyway." Eventually Father Bird had to agree: his mother was an intrusion, no couple could stand it for very long. The curt removal of her backdoor key — there had been a scene, it was most unfortunate — meant he now ate much less mashed potato which, as William said, was obviously a blessing.

Father Bird checks his watch: in the kitchen everything would be fine. The pheasants will keep for another fifteen minutes. The cufflink will not go in — curse it — he reaches for another pair from the tallboy but, of course the tallboy was gone just like his mother. It had to go: as William explained, it was huge and the colour of treacle, and where else could he fit the new exercise bike Father Bird had bought him? It made sense, of course it did, but Father Bird had liked that tallboy, if only because he could say.... An old joke. Never mind, he has a real tallboy of his own now. He tries the cufflink once again, it slips into place, and smoothing his hair he goes to greet his guests.

Downstairs in the drawing room William, Magnus and Toby are all comfortably seated, all holding fizzing glasses of champagne, and all apparently enjoying themselves enormously when Father Bird puts his head round the drawing room door.

"Lovely to see you!" he says.

"Smells delicious," says Toby.

"Is Graham coming?" asks Magnus.

"No, we haven't seen Graham for a while. Forgive me, boys, but I've a few birds that need me," and he darts down the hall towards the kitchen leaving a ripple of laughter behind him. Does he miss Graham? Well, perhaps a little. But it had been several months. "That venomous old lizard. He only ever wanted to get into my pants," William had said when they discussed whether Graham was to be on the guest list. It didn't matter, really. If it made William uncomfortable, then plainly Graham couldn't come.

The doorbell chimes again, but with oven-gloves on and the red-wine reduction to complete Father Bird has no choice but to listen as, once again, William performs the greeting. Two voices — he doesn't recognise them. This must be Darren and his boyfriend — ugly word, companion is so much preferable — his boyfriend, what was it, Steve? Friends of William. Father Bird has never met them before and glances round the kitchen door and down the hall for a quick look. He tells himself: perhaps they will be fun, despite everything, despite the trainers and the t-shirts and the rest of it. After all, you can't expect a young man of nineteen like William to spend his evenings with a load of dinosaurs.

The sound of music suddenly floods in from the drawing room — loud, strong bass line, contemporary, he's been told what it was but rock and pop and techno and — the entire vocabulary doesn't mean a thing to Father Bird. Voices are raised, he can hear William saying something and everyone laughing. Did he hear his name mentioned? He's not sure. He can smell cigarette smoke, too, or something at any rate that might have been cigarette smoke. For a moment, a daring giddy moment, he thinks he might dash into the party, throw open the piano, and join in — but they would scarcely welcome Chopin, not now, or even Richard Rodgers and Oscar Hammerstein. They are having fun in a way that he does not quite understand.

As he watches the sauce bubble gently Father Bird thinks: those trainers had very heavy treads — and the cigarette ash — should I worry about my floors? If I open a window tomorrow morning would it dispel that strangely herbal scent, which will be lingering in the upholstery?

Father Bird bends to open the oven door and as he does so catches a reflection in the oven's glass door. For a moment he thinks he sees his mother's anxious face looking him in the eye. For half a second he returns the look then opens the door and peers through the heat haze. Ten more minutes then it's ready, he decides. Time to go through, grab a glass, say hello?

From the drawing room comes the sound of wood against silver against carpet as an occasional table crashes to the floor. Over the pounding music surges a gale of screeching laughter. No, no, Father Bird says to himself as he checks the timer and folds his oven gloves, I'll stay right here, where I am.

Bless the young people, he says out loud, bless them all.

The Real World

"Paulie?" a voice is calling through the letterbox, "Paulie? It's Martin."

Paulie, wearing only dirty white socks and boxers, unlatches the front door then scampers back into the lounge and arranges himself on the settee with a magazine. Seconds later Martin is standing next to him, putting his briefcase on the floor and unzipping his coat.

"I'll hang it over a chair, shall I?" he asks, hanging it over a chair. Paulie turns the page and says nothing. Martin brushes some sawdust off the seat under the window next to the chinchilla cage and sits down heavily, resting the briefcase on his lap.

This morning the chinchillas are unhappy: there are wood shavings all over the carpet. Last night Paulie forgot to shut the blinds so, of course, the summer sun woke them at dawn and because there was no food left in their little trays they had kicked bedding and pellets everywhere.

Martin glances at the mess.

"Well," he says cheerfully, folding his fat hands on the briefcase. "Good to see you again Paulie." Paulie stares at his magazine, his attention fixed on a full-page picture of a young man in a dinner jacket arm in arm with a young woman in an ivory gown. The headline reads 'Adam and Stacey Scrubbed Up for Soap Awards.'

Martin opens the briefcase and pulls out a large pad of ruled writing paper and a ballpoint pen, both of which he arranges on his improvised desk before re-folding his hands, his smooth sausage fingers locked loosely together. "So," he says, "how's it been?"

Paulie does not appear to hear. Martin nods sympathetically.

"Tough, eh?" he says soothingly, and watching for a reaction or response notices how the morning sun is slanting through the venetian blinds so that a dozen narrow shadows fall diagonally across Paulie making him look as if he has been cancelled or crossed out. "Nice and bright in here, isn't it?" Martin says. "So, Paulie, these last few days. Have you been looking after yourself?" Pause. "Or have you been getting up at silly o'clock?"

Paulie is biting his lip. He could be reading, or he could just be studying the picture very carefully.

"You know why I've come, don't you Paulie?" Martin continues. "It's about last night. Last night and yesterday morning," he says, and as he does so he pulls a pink printed page from within the folds of his notebook. "Last night in particular," he says.

Suddenly Paulie is out of the chair and trying to snatch the piece of pink paper. Martin presses it firmly down onto his briefcase with his fat hands so that Paulie cannot grasp it, his fingers sliding off harmlessly. The chinchillas, panicking, send another shower of wood shavings onto the floor.

Paulie coils back onto the sofa, picks up the magazine, and opens it roughly. He stares at another picture — this time a heavily pregnant TV presenter pushing a shopping trolley across a car park. Only his slightly accelerated breathing records his failure.

"You know I can't show you the complaint, Paulie," says Martin, brushing a scattering of sawdust off the page. "Data protection."

Martin smiles and folds his hands.

"My guess is, looking around, that you've not totally been looking after yourself, like we agreed. My guess," he says, "is that you've been spending all your time thinking about Little Brad."

Paulie scratches his leg, working his way slowly down to the frayed elasticated ankles of his socks. All the time his eyes stay fixed on the photo spread.

"When we moved you here..." Martin begins to say, and then stops. He smiles again. "To be fair," Martin continues, "I see you've put up the picture you got from the day centre." He nods towards the large badly creased poster which has been blu-tacked to the middle of the wall. It shows an over-lit cave interior under the title Wookie Hole is Wonderful. It is the only decorative touch in a room of random unmatched furniture.

Martin unfolds his chubby white hands, and slaps them gently on the notepaper, as if closing a meeting or sealing a deal. "Ok," he says, opening the briefcase again and carefully replacing the paper, pen and pink printed sheet. Paulie glances up quickly and cautiously. "Ok, we'll talk off the record. Just you and me," says Martin.

He shuts the case, spins the combination lock, and places it carefully on the floor beside him, watching Paulie for reactions which do not come. "Let's start again," he says. "Paulie, we all have our problems. Take me and Roger. Roger turned forty, said he needed to think, and did most of his thinking in the gym. Now he has the body of an eighteen year old and says he's an erotonaut on a cosmic adventure." Martin stops to pick a small piece of sawdust from the shoulder of his shirt. "I hate to think what he's doing every night. I mean," he says. "I've had to put my emotional life in a box."

Conscious that he is being watched Martin turns to his left, and his gaze is met at roughly head-height by the two chinchillas, standing close-pressed side by side, one of them nibbling a piece of dried banana. "The truth is," says Martin, still looking at the chinchillas who are swiveling their ears attentively, "that we all learn to control ourselves. If you want to get up at four in the morning then that's fine, live and let live. But why go and knock on all the neighbours doors?"

Martin turns to address his final words to Paulie, to find that he too is watching the chinchillas. Paulie, discovered, fusses with his magazine, as if looking for the right page.

Martin continues: "I know you get worried sometimes about Little Brad. But the neighbours need their sleep. And you frighten them, especially some of the old ladies, if you say Little Brad's gone missing, and might be dead or run over. They don't understand when you call him your baby. People don't do this in the real world."

For a moment he pauses and examines Paulie, who is now looking past him through the blinds at the street. Opposite and all around are identical Manchester Corporation semi-detacheds.

Martin begins again: "The same goes for Little Angelina. And this isn't the first time, is it? You've been told before that you mustn't say that your baby boy is sick and dying at home. You've been told not to ring 999. I know you remember that. But you mustn't ask the neighbours to call 999 for you, OK? It is just as bad as if you'd called them yourself."

Martin can see that Paulie's lips are moving — he is mouthing something, or whispering very quietly.

Martin says: "Paulie? Paulie?" and then, loud and sharply, "Do. You. Understand. Question. Mark."

Martin's sudden unexpected change of tone upsets the chinchillas who race round the cage in a state of extreme and noisy agitation. Paulie throws the magazine to the floor and rushes to the cage. The chinchillas, now squealing furiously, are trying to climb under each other. As they scrabble yet more sawdust cascades onto the carpet.

"Paulie," Martin is saying, as he stands, "You will remember this time?"

Paulie, tenderly jiggling a finger through the bars towards the terrified chinchillas, shows no sign that he has heard.

"I shan't make this formal," says Martin. "I've said what I came to say."

Paulie ignores him.

"Paulie?" says Martin. There is no reply. Martin picks up his briefcase and collects his coat from the back of the chair. "I'll be going," he says. "Remember."

The front door shuts and Paulie watches Martin walk down the concrete path to the road. Only when Martin's car is pulling out into the Burnage traffic does Paulie turn on the television, damping the volume with a few taps on the remote control. Slowly, as if fearful of waking a sleeping child, he returns to the sofa. The chinchillas, standing side by side, their little chests heaving, follow him anxiously with their eyes before turning warily towards the soothing normality of the TV screen.

Paulie retrieves the splayed magazine from the floor, shakes off a few flakes of sawdust, and settles himself on the sofa. He begins to watch the television, occasionally glancing tenderly at the chinchillas, who are now pottering around their cage hunting for more pieces of dried banana.

Before long he is absorbed, trance-like, in the TV talk shows. And as Paulie watches the figures on the TV screen so the late morning sun streams through the blinds, and the shadows of the busy animals play silently on the wall behind him.

Looking at Jamie

Here comes the bride, all fat and wide, the door chime hums synthetically.

Jamie hears movement inside, a dog barking, someone approaching, then the front door opens on Roy, short and bearded and very ugly, swaying like a cabaret singer and miming: "See how she wobbles, rolling from side to side..." He pauses dramatically then, more or less on the beat: "Jamie? Lovely to see you. Come in out of that dreadful cold." Jamie edges into the hall with his school backpack. "Put that there," says Roy, flapping his hand towards the bottom of the stairs. "I've just made a brew," and he trots off down the corridor, his Mickey Mouse slippers scuffing the worn red carpet. "Don't mind Betty," he shouts cheerily over a renewed volley of barks. "She's deaf."

In the kitchen Roy points to a cheap pine table surrounded by an assortment of unmatched chairs each made luxurious by the addition of a large frilly cushion.

"Make yourself comfy," he says. The room smells of gas leaks and old Collie dog, dark clumps of whose hair are strewn across the floor and has accumulated in drifts in the sticky hard-to-reach corners.

"So," says Roy, dropping a teabag into a mug and flicking the kettle on, "first time in Manchester? What could be finer in the state of Carolina."

"Not the first time," says Jamie. "But first time living here."

"Well well," says Roy as he fills the mug with hot water. "I'm always happy to squeeze in a nice young man." He pads to the cupboard and reaches down a carton of UHT milk. "Got a boyfriend?" he asks.

"No," says Jamie. "Not yet."

"And you've got a job?" says Roy, biting open a corner of the carton. "Or is there a daddy somewhere who pays your rent?"

"Kitchen porter," says Jamie.

"Bless. No daddy then." Roy puts Jamie's tea on the table and pulls out a chair for himself. "You said you were nineteen?"

"Sixteen. Seventeen in January."

"Hot toffee," says Roy thoughtfully. "You'll make lots of friends."

Ten minutes later Roy unlocks the door to what was once a ground floor dining room and which will now be Jamie's. He waves him inside where it is cold and paper-curlingly damp. A pair of heavily condensation-damaged French windows frame the view of small sludge-coloured courtyard strewn with cheap white patio chairs.

"We were out there all summer," says Roy, "larking and what-not." He bends to turn on an electric fan heater which proceeds to wheeze the smell of fiercely burning dust. "This isn't a squat or a sleazy knocking shop," says Roy. "This is Old Trafford's finest. Rent, cash, Sunday evenings. You do your own cleaning. Don't eat or drink anything from my cupboard in the kitchen. And when you have gentleman friends back here you wash your sheets yourself. Roy doesn't wash crispy sheets." He flicks the ceiling light on and off in an experimental fashion. It blinks into life, which seems to surprise him, then he throws the key onto the bed. "Of course you could always get them to come in your mouth if you don't fancy doing the laundry," he says, and is gone.

Jamie puts his bag on the duvet and drops down next to it. Under the light of the bare bulb the room looks like a crime scene. He opens his backpack and pulls out a fist full of t-shirts and socks until he exposes a slim silver camera. He lifts it out and presses the on-button so that the lens whirs out of its machined-smooth surface. Jamie holds the camera in front of him and pans it round the room, watching this new panorama on the camera's miniature screen: a boarded-up Victorian fireplace, its cast iron chipped and re-painted countless times; a tired chest of drawers; thin sun-bleached curtains; black grime in the corners of the window panes. He leans back, points it at the French windows, and presses the shutter.

.

The first night: shifts mean it is gone two in the morning by the time Jamie gets home. He unlocks his bedroom door, tugs the curtains together, kicks off his Nikes. His clothes are greasy, dense with the odour of over-boiled vegetables and dirty grill pans, and his hands are raw with industrial-strength detergents. Above him on the first floor wardrobe doors are being banged shut and occasional busy footsteps are moving from one side of the room to the other. There is the indistinct bass-beat of music.

Jamie heads up to the bathroom and by the time he reaches the top of the stairs the music has resolved itself into something dancey and vaguely Latin. In front of him are three doors: one, firmly shut, leads to what Roy calls his "suite" carved out of the large front bedroom; another to the bathroom; the third is discretely open and it is from here that the music is shimmering like a warm night in Rio. A voice calls from inside: "You going to be long in there?"

"Five minutes," says Jamie.

"That's good," says the voice, "I need a shower." A tall thin heavily tanned figure inadequately wrapped in a small red hand-towel emerges from the room, not quite prancing but almost. Two paces out the towel drops to the floor revealing a body shaved and hairless. He assumes a face of outraged decency. "You rough boys!" the man says, holding his hands up theatrically, "Why'd you try to steal my towel?" He makes no attempt to cover himself and simply smiles. "I am Tadeo," he says, "and you are Jamie who is sixteen?" Jamie nods. "I thought so," he says, "Roy told me." Apparently satisfied with the impression he has created, Tadeo picks up the towel and drags it back into his room. "It's ok," he calls from inside. "I don't need the shower so much."

Tadeo appears in the kitchen late the following morning just as Jamie is making himself a mug of coffee. This time he is wearing a t-shirt and boxers. "Roy is still sleeping," Tadeo volunteers, turning on the radio. He puts a slice of bread into the toaster and dances sinuously whilst it browns, his bare feet disturbing the loose dog hair.

"That job you got," he says. "It's shit. Shit place. They have rats in the kitchen."

Jamie, sitting at the kitchen table with the camera placed neatly in front of him, shrugs and says: "It pays for my nights off."

"Party boy," says Tadeo, retrieving the toast. "Sexy party boy." He shimmies to the fridge and retrieves an enormous tub of margarine which he opens and sniffs, still wiggling vaguely. "You gonna take sexy pics of me?" he says, swinging himself round and scooping up the camera. He takes a seat opposite Jamie and, Spreading his toast with one hand he turns on the camera with the other; he scrolls through its memory. A series of images of Jamie — shirtless, happy, dancing — appear, his bright face surrounded by shimmering zig-zag smears of light. Then a change of tone: a single yellow glove on an a tartan-upholstered bus seat; a weak winter sun setting at the end of the long vista of the Stretford Road; a scattering of frosty cars abandoned outside the cinema at the Trafford Centre.

"Your friend took these?" says Tadeo. "The ones in the club," says Jamie, "I took the rest on Saturday."

Tadeo drops the camera on the table and concentrates on eating.

"Careful," says Jamie, snatching it away.

Tadeo takes no notice. "You need a sexy model like me," he says, "Roy likes to take pictures of me."

Jamie checks the camera for damage. It looks ok.

"You wanna come for a smoke?" says Tadeo, brushing crumbs from his t-shirt onto the floor. "Doors open all the time."

An hour later Jamie settles himself on the floor of Tadeo's room. It looks like someone is half-way through tidying it. A pair of white trousers are slung over the door, things spill out of draws. Tadeo, sitting cross-legged on the bed, has a huge glass ash tray balanced on one knee. Behind him, stuck to ancient roses-and-briars wallpaper, hangs a huge high-gloss Kylie poster. It has been ingeniously adapted: pasted over the place where her ears should have been were two generously erect penises, each carefully cut from a magazine. The result is strangely extraterrestrial.

"Roy fucked you yet?" says Tadeo, passing Jamie the joint. Jamie, inhaling, shakes his head vigorously.

"He'll try. He always tries."

Jamie holds his breath then releases the smoke in a neat narrow jet. Tadeo watches then reaches for the joint, and laying flat on the bed enjoys a luxurious drag. "So what is Jamie?" he asks at last.

"Jamie is chilling," says Jamie. Alien Kylie smooches down at him approvingly. Tadeo offers him the joint. " And smoking. And taking pictures," he says.

Tadeo points an imaginary camera at Jamie's groin. "Snappy snappy," he says.

.

Tap. Tap tap.

From outside in the back yard Jamie can hear scuffings and movings, as if plastic furniture is being re-arranged. He can also hear occasional words that don't quite add up to a conversation.

Tap tap.

 He keeps his eyes shut: late night, late shift, he isn't ready to get up.

"Jamie darling," Roy calls through the French windows and once again raps on the glass with his finger nails, "Coo-eeee." Another voice, presumably Tadeo's, says something which Jamie can not make out. There is a pause and the clinking of bottles. "It's a lovely day, Jamie," Roy adds in a queenly voice. The sound of conversation resumes and a radio, tuned to aggressively and inappropriately loud party-mood music, is turned on loud.

 Jamie swings himself out of bed, switches on the electric fan heater and from the pile of yesterday's clothes pulls a pair of jeans still smelling of the sweet-stale remains of the plate-scraping bins. He throws back the curtains and chilly January brightness floods in.

Seated next to one another on the now upright patio furniture are Tadeo and Roy. Both are wearing huge coats and sunglasses, having created in a corner of the wrecked yard a kind of makeshift poolside paradise. A umbrella with "Stella Artois" printed round the edge has been rammed into the hole once reserved for a rotary washing line. Magazines and cigarettes are strewn around the crazy paving; an over-powered portable sound-system sits between them and next to Roy's chair is a six-pack and two bottles of wine. Both men are holding a glass.

"Look," says Roy, turning towards the French windows. "Isn't she gorgeous."

Tadeo, sipping his pint under the heavy shade of the umbrella, lowers the drink just enough and squints in Jamie's direction. "You need some sun, sexy English boy," he shouts over the music. "Don't bother with a t-shirt."

"Come out here," says Roy, patting his lap encouragingly. Through the glass Jamie says: "I'm going into town. Take some pictures in the sun."

Roy affects not to hear, instead reaching down to a can of lager which he waves theatrically. "We've got boo-ooze," he explains. "Boy booze."

Jamie ducks out of sight then re-appears with his camera. "Smile" he shouts. Tadeo and Roy both assume film-star profiles and raise their glasses with poise. Click-shsh.

"I'll catch you later, ok?" says Jamie.

"Your loss," shouts Roy over the pounding disco beat, "fuck off then with your fucking camera," and he turns to Tadeo who says something, and they both laugh.

By four o'clock the sun is long gone: winter darkness has returned. Jamie can hear the music, still blasting, as he walks towards the house from his bus; from the inside it is clear that the volume has been turned to neighbour-insulting level, so loud it is distorted and unrecognisable. He follows the noise through the hall, and out into the yard where in the gloom the two patio chairs are on their sides, abandoned amidst empty cans and bottles. He finds the sound system and turns it off. As he walks to his room Tadeo calls from upstairs "Jamie you home? Jamie! Sexy boy!"

Heavy uncoordinated footsteps above are followed by Roy and Tadeo tumbling and giggling down the stairs.

"You turned the party off!" says Tadeo accusingly.

"Sweet sixteen and never been sucked," says Roy, close behind. "Now that I don't believe." Roy leans toward Jamie's face. "Go on," he says breathily. "Give your daddy a helping hand."

"He's pissed," says Tadeo.

"Can you get him out of here?" says Jamie.

"Roy's ok, just a bit you know. We missed you. You wanna come up stairs and watch a video?"

"I'm going to download this," Jamie says, indicating the camera still hooked round his wrist.

"Oh come on Jamie, come up with us, just ten minutes ok?" says Tadeo.

Roy's boudoir is dominated by a huge flat screen television in front of which sits an equally enormous black leather sofa.

"You'll like it," says Roy, crouching on the floor in front of the DVD player, "It's new. Sort of costume drama."

Tadeo arranges himself confidently at one end of the sofa, and Jamie sits on the floor, as the disc slow-mos through copyright warnings and a series of rainbow-coloured producers' logos. Then the titles of the film begin to roll: over pictures of modern-looking boys carrying satchels and wearing grey school shorts it says Oliver Twink, by Charles Dick-ins, the next frame adding in campy copperplate Or A Tale of Two Twinkies. Roy kicks off his Mickey Mouse slippers, tucks his legs up on the sofa, and leans over Jamie. "Tell me," he says, breathing stale white wine, "have you ever considered a career in porn?" Jamie pulls an as-if face.

Roy starts to hum "I am sixteen coming on seventeen."

.

Jamie wakes late in his own bed. He has no idea how long he has been asleep: a thin light leaks through the curtains. Upstairs he can hear Roy and Tadeo screeching over what sounds like heavily amplified porn. A door opens, feet thud across the landing, toilets flush and amidst more giggling the door to Roy's suite shuts again. Jamie rolls to the edge of the bed, reaches down to the floor, and soon finds his camera.

Laying on his back and holding the camera above his head, Jamie toggles through the images: Tadeo and Roy in the backyard looking slutty; Manchester Town Hall clock tower seen from different angles; the crowds in Market Street, girls swinging Primark bags, lads strutting in gangs; then the winter sun reflected in the windows of a King Street office block.

From Roy's boudoir comes the sound of excited barking and, amidst more laughing, the thump of something heavy falling over. More footsteps rush back and forward as if a crazy chase were in progress. Betty the dog is howling, confused by the movement and vibrations.

Jamie scrolls again, expecting to be returned to the picture of Tadeo and Roy. But instead a new and unforeseen image appears: Jamie asleep in his bed, his eyes shut. Jamie studies the image carefully, noticing his messed-up hair, the way one arm flops over the quilt, his head to one side, his mouth slightly open. He presses the scroll button again and a second image appears. It is just as before, only the duvet has been thrown back to show him sprawled on his back on the thin under sheet. His boxers are twisted round his waist. Just visible across his body are two shadows.

Jamie scrolls forward and a third image appears. The composition is exactly like the others: Jamie is on his back, on the bed, asleep, eyes firmly shut. But this time his boxers have been tugged down to his ankles and a pair of Mickey Mouse slippers have been more or less arranged on his feet.

Above him Roy's boudoir bursts open releasing a gale of disco music. There is barking and confusion as Betty escapes and is then returned and locked inside. Footsteps can be heard on the landing. Excited giggling is accompanied by the heavy creaking of the wooden stair treads as Roy and Tadeo lurch down. Outside Jamie's room the tittering is replaced by clumsy shushing and whispered conversation.

There is a pause.

The handle begins to move.

Jamie puts the camera to his eye, points it at the door, and begins to frame his image.

The New Union

"Epics embody the history and aspirations of the
peoples/nations they tell of....."

J.A. Cuddon, *The Penguin Dictionary of Literary Terms*

Sing, oh muses! Sing of Mancunia, god of this place, thrice-
blessed by your daughter nymphs, the naiads of the purling
Medlock, the crystal Irk, and the refreshing Irwell.

Sing of the rain and of the pavements freckled with chewing
gum, of chips with curry sauce and discount sportswear
retailers. From your holy home high on Cheetham Hill descend
and sing, dear ladies, of the slow moving buses, bumper to
bumper on the majestic Oxford Road, and of the regimented
café tables of Canal Street. For this, surely, is a well-watered
vale of the Muses, and every thing in it an archive of your
works.

Foremost amongst those works is The New Union, a temple
erected over a reviving fountain and dedicated to all nine
muses, but especially sacred to weeping Melpomene, laughing

Thalia and hectic Terpsichore. Descend with us tonight, oh muses, descend as that venerable pub's dance floor fills with the bearers of new t-shirts and old expectations; descend as the beats per minute accelerate and youthful hearts of all ages race to catch them. Descend in particular on the young man standing alone by the pillar, the one studying his mobile with anxiety, the one with half-empty glass and the slightly geeky haircut, for he deserves your blessing more than most. Behold, our hero. Hercules.

.

It's nine-ish and Andy has been standing there for about half an hour. He's made his lager last as long as possible and sent half a dozen texts, most of them inconsequential. His mates from work know that when he sends this kind of message — "hi — what year did Rick Astley reach number one??" — it means he's standing on his own in a bar waiting for someone. They send jokey replies: "thought early Kylie was more your kind of thing" or "has he stood you up?". If he doesn't get a reply to his original text within a few minutes Andy resends the text to another number or switches his iPhone over to Gaydar to see whose around in the world of gay virtual dating. He glances at the screen which reveals, not surprisingly, that there are 250 users within 100 metres. But he keeps his status set to "appear offline" — he doesn't want to get involved in anything new, not now. Not tonight. He re-sends the Rick Astley text to yet another number.

For a Wednesday it's busy in the Union and hardly anyone notices Andy's mimeshow of long-distance digital sociability. There's the usual crowd of Levenshulme lesbians, some older guys, thirty something couples having a drink before moving on somewhere else, students, a few screaming teens from the northern suburbs and a handful of suits who haven't yet made it onto their buses to West Didsbury or Chorlton. At no point in its seventy years as a gay venue — a village landmark long before the Village was ever dreamed of — has the Union been a trendy place, the height of queer chic. That was never its appeal. Too pokey, too provincial. Andy wouldn't have chosen it as a place to meet — indeed, he didn't tonight. He's here by appointment.

He'd suggested somewhere else. "Even Via would be better," he'd pleaded yesterday online, but seconds later a burst of staccato gunfire announced a reply from screen name: Hylas. No, Via wouldn't be better — it would be worse — they should choose the authentic tat of the Union over the styled fake tat of the newer bars. Not an untypical reply: their online encounters, maturing rapidly over about a week from the first "hi mate, nice picture" to the discovery of a catalogue of shared enthusiasms, always had an edge to them. Agreement on any topic wasn't immediate. There was always a qualification or a hesitation or a downright rejection. Andy had the sense that behind the profile — behind its photograph of young guy on a pool-side sun lounger lazily reading a copy of *AutoTrader* that teasingly hid all but his smiling eyes — there was someone pushing back. It was a nice feeling — an unusual feeling — this encounter with a self-contained personality. It was enough to justify a date.

His mobile melodiously announces a newly-received text. He checks the screen: "1986," it says, curtly. This reply is definitely not an invitation to exchange witty banter. Andy deletes it. Maybe try someone else. Or maybe go home, and give up this wait which his becoming rather a trial? On balance, he decides not. At least, not yet. Strange, though. Hylas didn't seem like the kind of guy for a no-show.

"You really need a haircut," says a voice next to him. Without lifting his eye from the mobile Andy replies: "Piss off Marcus."

"I'm only trying to be helpful," says the other, "It's getting rather Richard Chamberlain from Thorn Birds." He puts his glass down next to Andy's. "Do you like the t-shirt?" he adds, pushing his chest out. The slogan reads 'MOTHERS ADORE ME'

Still not looking up from the mobile Andy says: "I doubt it." This is how he likes to behave with Marcus, his neighbour in their terrace of small newly-built starter homes in Hulme. A little distant scorn helps to maintain a sense that although they live next door, and share the same failing misted-up double-glazing and cardboard walls, they are from quite different worlds.

"That scary bloke moved out, yet?" Andy asks.

"Roger? God yes," says Marcus, of his latest failed lodger-cum-lover.

"What was all that noise on Saturday night?"

"That was the final straw," says Marcus. "He put his sling and harness in the washer-dryer. It nearly started a fire." He gestures towards Andy's glass. "Fancy another?" (Andy nods yes) "Anyway, I've decided I don't need a lodger — I can survive without the money."

"Go back to the bingo-calling?" says Andy.

"Wythenshawe's best," says Marcus. "Back in a jiffy."

The late evening crowd is gradually replacing the after-work drinkers. A few Chinese lads are making whooping noises in front of the games machine; an immensely tall transvestite is stooping at the bar, demurely ordering a Campari. Someone calls "Estelle!" and she turns, smiling sweetly. No sign, though, of screen name: Hylas. A nice looking lad, so far as you could tell from the pictures he'd emailed. Another, same poolside scene, only with *Auto Trader* on the ground. Blonde, smiling, relaxed, a tidy-looking guy in red Speedos; and a third, a handsomely moody Magnum-style silhouetted profile which was either very cleverly thought-out and professional, or a happy digital-camera accident. Imperfections? Maybe he was a bit short — but that could be the effect of the camera angle. Anyway, not short enough to drop him. Not freakishly small. Side-by-side they wouldn't look like Winnie-the-Pooh and Piglet holding hands. Hopefully.

Marcus returns, handing over Andy's new pint whilst taking a slurp from his own.

"Who you waiting for, then?" he asks.

"A friend," says Andy.

"I see," says Marcus.

They stand silent for a moment.

"You seen the girls moved in down the road?" says Marcus.

"On Sunday afternoon? Blue estate car?"

"That's them, no van or nothing. Lesbians don't believe in possessions," says Marcus.

There is another silence.

"Right," Says Marcus. "Catch you later."

Still no sign of screen name: Hylas. Puzzling. They swapped mobile numbers last night: a sign of trust and a kind of proof that the date was real. He checks the Gaydar app again: Hylas is listed online. This is weird, or humiliating, or both. Would it be ok to text? Or would that be bad? And what would he say anyway: "Where the hell are you?" like some old married couple? Or, much much worse, "Are you ok? I was worried." The number is already programmed into his address book — under Hylas because, too careless or too cool, he hasn't yet asked for his real name. He opens utilities > address book > change entry — then pauses. He opens a new message, keys "Are you on your way?" and presses send.

Uncomfortable, he feels uncomfortable. The latest dumb-show on the phone has drawn attention to his solitary watch by the pillar, and not in a good way. Glances which seconds ago he interpreted as approving now make him want to blush because he is being redefined, moved from the category of lone wolf on the prowl (desirable, sexy) to needy guy looking for someone to cling to (sad, potential stalker)? The blush — the blush that comes as he checks his mobile again and adjusts his posture, foot against the wall, genuine-bloke look — is recognition that it might be the latter. The truth is that all day he has been preparing himself for this evening. This morning the bus journey into town and the walk across Albert Square, down Brazennose Street to the office off Deansgate was almost over before he realised he'd been improvising conversations between himself and Hylas, imagined points of contact expanded into fully worked-out scripts. And at work, he'd had his mobile next to him on the desk, logged in at Hylas's profile, watching the device's periodic updates. By the time he got home — suit back on its hanger, tie unknotted and draped over the back of a chair — he'd had plenty of time to decide what to wear this evening: good jeans, nice white Oxford shirt, slate-grey jacket, his good watch and a quality belt. Call it professional-preppy he said, gelling his hair in the mirror. Finished and satisfied he took a final look: armed for battle he said, as he says to himself every night before he goes out.

That was earlier. Now it's just a total anxiety situation. Still no reply. Radio silence from Hylas. Andy studies the now loud and lively pub: have I missed him, did he walk in, not find me, think I'd stood him up and left? Or did he see me and I was a let down — much worse than he expected? Or is he here somewhere, leaning against a pillar of his own, waiting for me and wondering why I'm so late? He checks his mobile again. Hylas is still online. Why not — nothing ventured: "Where the hell are you?" he keys, then pauses a moment, erases "the hell", and presses send.

Hell indeed is what he is imagining. He is saying to himself: If Hylas doesn't appear in five minutes I'll buy another pint — then maybe I'll go and sit with Marcus for a while. If he asks about tonight I'll make some joke about time-wasters. A fourth pint, perhaps, tank up here because it's cheaper than in a club, and about half eleven follow the crowd down the street to Essential. Down the stairs, into the underworld.

■

High up on Cheetham Hill the great god Mancunia stirs and as he stirs the entire city trembles: a surge in the power supply flutters the neon signs outside the Indian restaurants of the Wilmslow Road; the bamboo planted around the Chinese pavilion on George Street chatters as if a caught in a sudden breeze; the fountain in Albert Square appears to pause, water frozen in mid-air, before resuming its fall with heavy splashes;

the banners hanging from the portico of the Central Library snap furiously, as if ripped from their moorings, then as suddenly drop limp and weightless. At tram stops and bus stops, street corners and doorways, on pavements and in takeaways all remark without being able quite to explain it the sudden revival of a feeling, neither good nor bad but as natural here as the rain, a feeling with which they are all familiar: something is about to happen. Quite suddenly every street light, shop sign and bar within three miles of Piccadilly is plunged into darkness.

Mancunia wakes and calls to him his fairest and youngest daughter, Medlock, nymph of the southern river. Shy Medlock, he says yawning and stretching, discrete and dearest Medlock, what have you been doing, for I have a feeling you have been doing something? Father, she says, I could not help it. I saw a beautiful youth and a jealous passion overwhelmed me. For a moment the air fills with the static of approaching thunder, the sky grows dark and low, and the city trembles again. But the storm does not come. Oh silly but forgivable girl, says Mancunia, was he comely and handsome? Medlock nods, fearing to meet her father's eyes. Mancunia smiles and asks: was it Hylas you saw? Medlocks nods again. Mancunia shakes his head silently. You take after me, you wonderfully superficial girl, he says. You had better tell me everything. Medlock, relieved, begins to explain. She says: I saw him walking up the Oxford Road, hurrying to meet his Hercules. First I delayed him by sending two dozen slow-moving students at All Saints. But he weaved through the students. Next I sent a convoy of buses to make it impossible for him to cross the Oxford Road. But he was patient, and daring, and managed to cross. Finally, fearing that he would escape from me, I commanded the west wind to take the form of the slip-stream of a fast-moving Number 42 which knocked him off balance just as he was crossing my bridge by the Refuge building. I hoped, Medlock continues, that Hylas would fall into my arms but.... and she shows her father a small white rectangular object the screen of which reads, through distorting drops of brackish water, "New message received." And so, she concludes, this little loveless thing fell into the water instead. Mancunia stands and scratches his perpetually itching crotch. Interfering but loveable girl, says Mancunia, this object may be more important than you think, and must be returned. Nymphs have ways, and you must use them. If he calls a third time my Hercules shall have his Hylas, for is it not decreed that, where I rule, all who ask are heroes and that none who ask shall be denied?

■

The dance music in the New Union has resumed after the unexpected fusing of the entire electrical system throughout central Manchester. The lights on the games machines are flashing again and the Chinese lads are beginning where they left off. At the bar the pumps are flowing. The immensely tall transvestite is sharing a laugh with a small but exquisitely dressed clergyman. In the momentary confusion caused by darkness and silence carefully created poses have been disarranged and well-prepared attitudes unfrozen. A general giddy conversation has broken out.

"Just like the blitz," says Marcus. "Anybody give you a squeeze in the dark?"

"Not a soul," says Andy.

"Talking of which, where is your date?" says Marcus.

"I don't know," says Andy. Then, making a confession which he is aware he could not and would not have made had it not been for the sudden relaxation caused by the power cut, he adds: "I think I've been stood up."

Andy thinks: is that it then, is the evening over? Disappointed and now humiliated, duped and dumped and not even drunk, it can't really get worse. He will go home, he will look at Hylas' profile for the last time and delete the it from his list of favourites. He will go to bed. He will be brave. Andy flips open his mobile for what he tells himself will be the last time today. It is just as he expected: nothing, no missed calls, no new texts, no echo from the world. Yet next to his profile Hylas is still listed as online.

Marcus snatches the phone.

"Who's this then," he says, looking at the picture of Hylas. "You're dating a copy of *Auto Trader*. Typical."

"Give it back," says Andy, and then wishes he hadn't because it sounds very uncool.

"What's behind the magazine?" asks Marcus, examining the profile photo, and as he does so turning his back on Andy to make sure he's out of retaliatory phone-grabbing range. "Hang on," he says, turning back, "I think I can guess. Behind the *Auto Trader* there's a copy of *What Caravan?* And behind that a copy of *Exchange and Mart*."

Andy drinks from his lager and, over the foam, scans the room.

Marcus continues: "You'll suit one another perfectly. You can share erotic fantasies about the re-sale values of Ford Cortinas." He chooses the menu and ostentatiously selects the sent box.

"So what have you two been saying to one another?" he says.

"Please Marcus," says Andy. "Give it back."

"Just a moment," says Marcus, turning again. He scrolls through the list of sent messages: What year did... What year did.... What year did.... R u on... Where r u?

"I suppose it has been quite a dull evening," he says handing the phone back, "I blame myself."

The tall transvestite is now standing in front of the poker machine deeply embedded amongst the crowd of Chinese lads. There is a sudden whoop of congratulation and a sparkly clutch-bag is momentarily in the air above her head.

Perhaps it is the sense of shared intimacy created by the power cut, perhaps it is because Marcus has uncovered too many secrets already: either way, Andy feels confessional. He wants to explain to someone that he's getting bored with searching, and that his strength and courage are beginning to fail him. There have been too many battles to get served at the bar, too many perilous journeys to the toilets, too many visits to the Hades of the basement nightclubs. He is too old for all this, and his jeans and jacket feel like antique armour, armour that is becoming too heavy for him to carry.

And a thought occurs. Nothing ventured, nothing gained. Perhaps the gods will be kind. He selects the last message he sent to Hylas (where r u?) and presses send. Send to Hylas? the screen asks. Andy presses confirm.

All around him little victories are being won: on the far side he can see Marcus, pressed onto a banquette with one of the stray office workers who has now lost his jacket; the giggling

Blackley teenagers appear to be chasing one of the Chinese lads round the dance floor. Men and women are mixing and mingling, mincing and moaning, making love and making moves, just like they do every night of the week.

Somewhere very close to him Andy can hear a ring tone announce the arrival of a message. It is a strange little tune, something vaguely traditional and simultaneously exotic, perhaps played on zithers. You might almost call it Greek. The phone's owner stops the ring tone and makes a sound that Marcus would certainly call a titter. Almost immediately Andy's own phone springs into life. New message received. It reads simply: "Turn round."

He turns.

"Hylas," says Andy, surprised.

For there he was.